CRIMINAL MINDS

CORNWALL COLLEGE
LEARNING CENTRE

CRIMINAL MINDS

David Owen

Grange
BOOKS

A QUANTUM BOOK

Published by Grange Books
an imprint of Grange Books Ltd
The Grange
Kingsnorth Industrial Estate
Hoo, nr, Rochester
Kent ME3 9ND
www.grangebooks.co.uk

ISBN: 978-1-84804-003-8

This book was produced by
Quantum Publishing Ltd
6 Blundell Street
London N7 9BH

QUMPSYC

Project Editors: Ruth Patrick, Duncan Proudfoot, Corinne Masciocchi
Art Director: Roland Codd
Designer: James Lawrence
Creative Director: Richard Dewing
Associate Publisher: Laura Price
Publisher: Oliver Salzmann

Printed in Singapore by
Star Standard Industries (Pte) Ltd

With special thanks to Rosie Barry at Quintet Publishing for her invaluable assistance
with picture research; Allison Limbrick Barkley at Rome-Floyd County Public Library,
Rome GA; Cheryl Fontaine at King County Library System, Bellevue WA; Barbara Moss
at the Newark Star Ledger, Newark NJ; Karen Valentine; Laura Conerly at the
Noel Memorial Library at LSU in Shreveport, Shreveport LA; Katie Schrimpf at
The Hayner Public Library District, Alton IL; Lieutenant John Lakin, Chief of Detectives,
Madison County Sheriff's Office, Madison County IL.

Foreword

IN THE RELATIVELY BRIEF PERIOD since the foundation of the first police forces and other crime-fighting agencies, the application of science to the identification of individual criminals has become a powerful and sophisticated weapon for the maintenance of law and order. From the development of fingerprinting to the discovery of DNA as a means of identifying a single individual from the smallest traces of bodily material, a wide range of methods exists to prove a particular suspect was in fact the perpetrator of a given crime. In cases where motive, means, and opportunity suggest a prime suspect, or range of suspects, forensic science can often establish guilt or innocence to a high degree of accuracy and reliability.

But what about those cases which defy rational deduction? Police statistics show, for example, that most cases of homicide are the handiwork of a close family member — or sometimes a close business associate — carried out for clear personal reasons. Even where several suspects could all have had powerful motives for wanting the victim dead and the opportunity to translate their wishes into actions, the identification of these potential suspects remains a logical and containable process. With a combination of careful questioning to check alibis and witnesses, and the use of forensic laboratory technology to read the traces found at the crime scene, the truth is likely to be relatively accessible through a process of classic police detective work.

In a minority of high profile cases, though, there is little logical connection between killer and victim. Homicides may result from the most casual and unexpected of encounters, with nothing to link the murderer with his or her prey beyond their presence in the wrong place at the wrong time. Serial killers, for example, form a terrifying group which is largely, though not entirely, confined to affluent Western societies. Driven by such arbitrary and irrational impulses, they remain the most elusive targets for the forces seeking to track them down. Because that first step of identifying and tracking down the potential suspects becomes the most difficult of all, there is a real danger that the investigation can remain stalled at this preliminary obstacle.

It was to help law-enforcement agencies to bridge this gap that the techniques of crime analysis and profiling were first developed. While crimes may be too random and personal to respond to the classic motive-means-opportunity analysis, the criminal involved will still have definite motives for committing the crimes — however bizarre to the rational mind — and the means and the opportunity will reveal far more about the criminal, their background, their history, and other aspects of their personality than they would ever realize. By studying the victim of the crime, the scene where the crime took place, the weapon used to subdue or kill the victim, and the degree of injuries inflicted before or after death, profilers can determine a great deal about the kind of person responsible for the crime. In cases of serial crimes of violence, the criminal reveals more and more about his or her own personality with each succeeding case. Even the locations of the crimes can reveal their own pattern, sometimes helping to narrow down the area where the criminal lives, and takes refuge between one crime and the next.

The information which can be derived from studying all these factors is astonishing to the lay person. Skilled and experienced profilers can suggest the age and level of education of the as yet completely unknown criminal. They can pinpoint likely events in the criminal's personal history from the kind of petty crimes they may have committed earlier in their career to their relationship with their parents, their sexual experience and their military service, the kind of work they are likely to do, and the probable make and even the color of the car they drive. In some cases, not all these details may prove to be 100% accurate in the case of the criminal who is finally arrested, charged, and convicted for the crimes. Nevertheless, in most cases the degree of correlation between the profile and the criminal is little short of staggering.

Criminal Minds takes the reader on a voyage of discovery into the challenging world of the criminal profilers. Succeeding chapters set out to illustrate different aspects of how profiling works. One covers the study of the crime scene and another the way in which the profile is prepared. Others describe the different types of criminals whose work is studied by profilers, and how they reveal themselves by the details of the crimes they commit — organized or disorganized criminals, commuters or marauders, abductors or abusers, kidnappers or extortionists. In addition, a series of classic true-crime, factual case studies shows how the work of individual profilers helped to identify the personality of the criminal responsible in landmark investigations, and to steer the search in the right direction to ensure ultimate success. It shows the interested lay reader how effective the thinking of profilers has been in the increasingly urgent and effective fight against ever more violent and unpredictable criminals.

David Owen

Introduction

T HE ART OF THE CRIME ANALYST AND PROFILER has become one of the most popular themes of current crime fiction, including both television programs and major feature films like *The Silence of the Lambs* and *The Bone Collector*. Seen through the lens of these fictional treatments, these experts appear as a modern-day Sherlock Holmes, able to use Holmes' shrewd powers of observation and knowledge of human nature to track down a violent criminal through the powers of the mind. While it was no coincidence that Holmes' creator, Sir Arthur Conan Doyle, was himself trained as a doctor and based his most famous fictional characters on one of the teachers at his Edinburgh medical school, the truth is that the work of the crime profiler differs most sharply from that of even forensic medical experts in two important respects.

In most cases, crime profiling helps to narrow down the search for a suspect by drawing conclusions from the crimes he has committed which enable a profile of the offender to be drawn up. This will cover his likely background, family history, intelligence, educational record, possible employment, race, marital status, hobbies and interests, and even the area in which he lives. All these can help the police focus their search more accurately, but they will not directly identify the perpetrator of the crimes in the classic Sherlock Holmes' manner.

BELOW
The cannibal serial killer Dr. Hannibal Lecter, played by Anthony Hopkins in the movie *The Silence of the Lambs* is perhaps the best known fictional target of a criminal profiler.

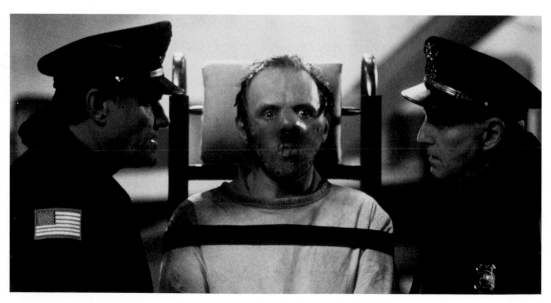

Also, because profilers are helping to narrow down the search from the impossibly wide target of the general population, they are still dealing with potentially large groups of likely suspects. This means that much profiling work may be of little use in terms of evidence at a trial — the profiler's role tends to be limited to helping to steer an investigation in the right direction initially, and narrowing down the search to a small enough target for traditional police methods to be successful in tracking down and identifying the prime suspect. From that point onward, the police have to provide the evidence which will convict the criminal before a court, and it is here that other specialists, from experts in ballistics to experienced practitioners in forensic medicine, have their vital contribution to make.

ABOVE
Dr. Arthur Conan Doyle, creator of Sherlock Holmes, who used insights into human behavior derived from his medical training to explain his hero's incredible deductions and abilities.

An additional difference between crime analysis and profiling and other techniques used to identify suspects and provide vital evidence is that this technique is relatively new. With one important exception, the experts who developed the techniques and proved their usefulness are part of the present day crime-fighting world rather than the historic past. In relatively recent memory, the natural suspicion of traditionally-minded investigating officers toward apparently speculative and unproven contributions from academic experts had to be overcome. For many of those officers, confident in their experience and ability in the established techniques of detection and investigation, the idea of 'reading' a crime scene to produce conclusions which would help catch the criminal seemed to be on a par with calling in psychics and spiritualists to communicate with the world of the criminals, or their victims.

Victorian London — and Jack the Ripper

The first ever criminal profile was drawn up more than a century ago, in a city which was gripped by fear resulting from the horrific revelations of one of the earliest and most notorious serial killers in criminal history. The city was London, the killer was the shadowy but terrifying figure of Jack the Ripper, and the time was 1888. In the mean streets of Whitechapel, in London's East End, an intricate network of slum alleys and overcrowded tenements, a series of five female murder victims had been discovered, suffering from progressively more violent mutilations. The first body was that of 42-year-old prostitute Mary Ann "Polly" Nichols, discovered by two market porters in a gateway off an alley called Buck's Row in the early morning of August 31st. Her throat had been cut through almost to her spine and she had suffered a series of deep incisions to her abdomen.

In just over a week, the killer's second victim was found in the yard behind 29 Hanbury Street, some half mile away from the location where the first body had been found, and close to the busy Spitalfields fruit and vegetable market. Once again the victim's throat had been cut, so fiercely that the head had almost been severed from the body, and she had been disemboweled. Her womb was found to be missing, and some small-denomination coins were found at her feet. Her identity was established as Annie Chapman, a 45-year-old flower seller and part-time prostitute who had been seen alive just half an hour earlier, negotiating with a prospective client, by one of the lodgers in the adjoining house.

Three weeks later, on Sunday September 30, 1888, the Ripper struck again, this time leaving two victims of his terrible handiwork. The first was discovered in a gateway off Berners Street by a jewelry salesman returning home in the early hours in

FROM LEFT TO RIGHT
Three of Jack the Ripper's victims: Mary Ann "Polly" Nichols, Annie Chapman, and Elizabeth Stride. All died at the hands of Victorian England's most notorious serial killer.

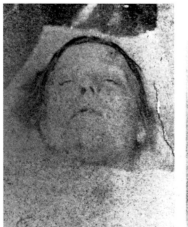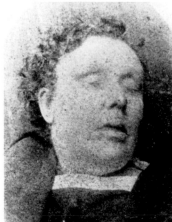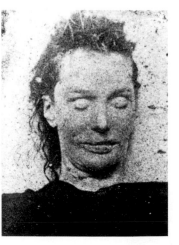

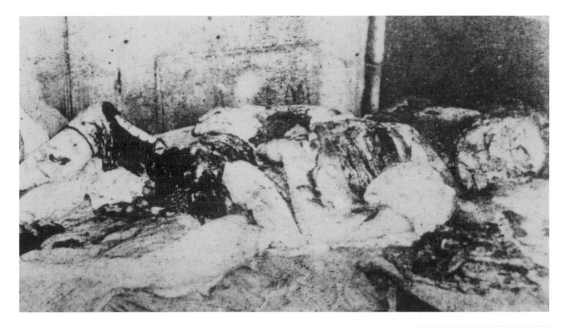

a pony and trap. The horse shied at a bundle lying on the floor, which he found to be the corpse of a woman, Elizabeth Stride. Once again her throat had been cut, but the body had not been mutilated, possibly because the arrival of the salesman had interrupted the killer. Whatever the reason, he struck again in Mitre Square, across the boundary of the City of London, in an area which was checked every quarter of an hour by a police constable on foot patrol.

Between two successive patrols, the Ripper had murdered his fourth victim, Catherine Eddowes, sometimes known as Kate Kelly. Ironically she had been arrested earlier for being drunk and incapable and been put in police cells at the nearby Bishopsgate station to sober up. She had been released at midnight and set out to walk back to her room, only to meet her killer on the way. In spite of the lack of time between visits from the police patrol, this time the Ripper had enough time to cut her throat and completely disembowel her.

The final murder in the series was discovered on the morning of November 9 after a break of a little over a month. The victim's body was found in a lodging house in Miller's Court, a few hundred yards away from the yard where the salesman's pony had recoiled in fear from Annie Chapman's corpse. One of the rooms had been let to 24-year-old prostitute Mary Jane Kelly, who had thrown her common law husband out after a fierce quarrel the night before. She had then spent the evening drinking and looking for customers, and a witness had seen her entering her room with a man just before midnight. It was a wet night, and some three to four hours later, a woman's voice crying "Oh, murder!" was heard over the sound of heavy rain.

Kelly had fallen behind with the rent for the room, and later the next morning the landlord's assistant called for the arrears. There was no reply to his knock on the door, but the window had been broken in the argument between Kelly and her husband the night before. The rent collector peered through the hole in the grimy pane to see her mutilated corpse on the bed within, with parts of her body hacked away and arranged on a bedside table.

The first criminal profile

At the time, conventional forensic science was in its infancy, but Dr. Thomas Bond, a police surgeon who carried out the autopsy on Mary Jane Kelly, was also asked to advise on whether the mutilations carried out on the bodies of the different victims showed definite evidence of surgical knowledge or experience. He also tried to reconstruct how the crimes had been committed, and considered what that might reveal about the person responsible. For example, he noticed that cuts in the bedsheet next to Mary Kelly's head and the fact that it was soaked with blood meant the killer could have used the sheet to cover her face at the time of the attack and avoid the danger of his clothes becoming bloodstained. This in turn made it possible that the killer took some care over his personal appearance, and he

"The whole of the surface of the abdomen & thighs was removed & the abdominal cavity emptied of its viscera. The breasts were cut off, the arms mutilated by several jagged wounds & the face hacked beyond recognition of the features. The tissues of the neck were severed all round down to the bone."
Excerpt from the autopsy on Mary Jane Kelly of Dr. Thomas Bond, the police surgeon

suggested the police should be on the look out for a respectably dressed middle-aged man, quiet and inoffensive in appearance.

Bond also examined the damage inflicted on the bodies of the earlier victims, and concluded that all the attacks had been carried out by the same person. This is another factor on which present-day profilers are often asked to give an opinion. On the question of whether or not the disemboweling showed the hand of a surgeon or at least someone with medical training, he concluded that the murderer not only had no scientific or anatomical knowledge, but also lacked the rudimentary knowledge of a butcher or even a slaughterman from one of the nearby slaughterhouses serving local butchers.

In reality, Bond's profile was never put to the test, and the real identity of the criminal known ever since as Jack the Ripper remains a mystery, though the horrific nature of the crimes and the meager but often conflicting pieces of evidence have maintained a high level of public interest ever since. One result of the failure to catch the killer, coupled with the fact that the murder of Mary Jane Kelly was the last of the Ripper killings, meant that this promising attempt to draw conclusions as to the identity of the killer from the evidence of his crimes remained an isolated example until well into the following century.

When it came, the next attempt to try to analyze the background and the psychology of a criminal was a very different case indeed. Instead of an anonymous serial killer with five individual victims on his record, the target of this new crime analysis was notorious throughout the world, responsible for actions which had cost the lives of millions. He was Adolf Hitler, dictator of Nazi Germany, which was then in the throes of World War II, with armies occupying most of Europe. Here the priority was not identification, but another important facet of crime analysis — prediction. Given that the subject was all too well known, what could crime analysis reveal about his attitudes, his priorities, and his likely actions when faced with a mortal threat?

Analyzing Hitler

The United States' Office of Strategic Services, the wartime predecessor of the Central Intelligence Agency (CIA) asked an experienced psychiatrist named Walter Langer to provide them with an analysis of the Nazi leader. Their main objectives were to find what his chief ambitions were, and how these might influence his direction of the war. In addition, as events were beginning to turn in favor of the Allies, this would put Hitler under increasing pressure. What, they wondered, would be the effect on Hitler's attitudes and policies? Finally, if they succeeded in capturing him in the final phase of the war, what would the analyst suggest would be a suitable strategy for them to follow in questioning him on his crimes?

Much of what Langer suggested was borne out by events. But the most successful prediction contained in the analysis was his estimate of how the Führer would meet his end. Langer assumed that death from natural causes or disease was unlikely over such a relatively short time span, particularly since Hitler was believed to be in good health. He also rejected the idea that Hitler might escape from a collapsing Germany and seek refuge in a friendly but neutral country. Because it was clear to him that Hitler saw himself as the savior of Germany, Langer was convinced that he would equate approaching defeat with death. After considering, and rejecting, the possibilities of death in battle, or assassination by political opponents like those responsible for the bomb plot of July 20, 1944, he suggested the most likely outcome would be that Hitler would commit suicide at the last possible moment to avoid capture by Allied troops. At the end of April 1945, Hitler proved Langer right when he shot himself in his bunker during the final Battle for Berlin.

ABOVE
The chaos in Hitler's Berlin bunker after its capture by the Allies in 1945. Hitler himself had proved the OSS analysis right by committing suicide rather then face capture by the Red Army.

After the war, crime analysis was used against enemy leaders in other campaigns, including the Vietnam War and, most recently, during the Gulf War of the early 1990s. But the use of analysis and profiling against criminals was only developed on an organized basis much later. The first case which showed the usefulness and the uncanny accuracy of a careful profiling was the investigation to track down the person responsible for the "Mad Bomber" blasts in New York city during the 1940s and 1950s (*see* Case study 1, page 19).

Later, similar ideas had occurred to other American police forces. An investigator named Howard Teten, working for the San Leandro Police Department in California, had begun using the expertise of psychologists from the School of Criminology at the University of California to help him narrow down his searches for the perpetrators of otherwise particularly insoluble crimes. In 1962, Teten moved to the Federal Bureau of Investigation (FBI) as a Special Agent, where in 1970 he began teaching a course in Applied Criminology at the FBI Academy at Quantico in Virginia. After detailed discussions with Dr. James Brussel, the profiler of the "Mad Bomber" in 1972, Teten used Brussel's highly effective method to teach other agents the value of profiling, and how to carry it out effectively.

LEFT
The FBI Academy at Quantico in Virginia, where methods of profiling were first developed, and the Behavioral Science Unit was established.

The start of FBI profiling

This pioneering initiative would soon lead to the establishment of the Behavioral Science Unit at the Academy, which covered profiling along with other criminal-psychologically-based areas of expertise like hostage negotiation and abnormal aspects of human behavior, taught by another BSU pioneer, Pat Mullany. In particular, Teten was able to demonstrate how the offender's behavior could be deduced from the evidence left at the scene of a crime, which became the cornerstone of FBI profiling policy. Serving police officers from different forces all over the U.S. attended the courses, and the experts were willing to advise on individual cases. FBI agent and lecturer John Douglas recalled one query from a California policeman to Howard Teten about the murder of a woman where the body showed repeated knife wounds. After studying the meager evidence available, Teten said they should look for a slightly built, unattractive teenager living not far from the victim's home, who had almost certainly killed her on an impulse, and who would be racked with guilt.

LEFT
George Metesky, the so-called "Mad Bomber" of New York after being caught and arrested at his home, faces up to life behind bars – later, he admitted to planting 32 bombs in different parts of the city.

One of the profiler's greatest advantages from the police point of view is being able to give advice on how to approach the suspect when identified. In this case, Teten said the individual's guilt would be so crippling that the best approach would be to knock on his door and when the suspect answered, simply to say "You know why I'm here." In his opinion, the shock would trigger an almost instant confession. In fact, the truth was even more remarkable. After house-to-house enquiries at the addresses of likely suspects in the area, one teenager who fitted the profile answered the door to the policeman's knock with the words "Okay, you got me!"

The fame of the BSU soon spread and the idea of profiling as a powerful aid in apprehending violent criminals became increasingly accepted by police forces looking for help in solving bloody and highly publicized murder cases. To improve the level of their knowledge of how criminals' minds worked, several BSU members conducted lengthy interviews with convicted serial killers and rapists in U.S. prisons. These produced more valuable information which helped produce more accurate and more detailed profiles, and from the late 1970s onward, public recognition of the value of criminal profiling became much more widespread. Finally, in 1985, the Behavioral Science Unit was absorbed into the National Center for the Analysis of Violent Crime (NCAVC) which was set up at the Quantico Academy. From this point on, profiling was seen as an essential weapon in the police armory against violent and disturbed criminals.

All the profile subjects in this introduction and its associated case study are men. Indeed, in the vast majority of cases reviewed in this book, it will become all too apparent that the perpetrators are male. In a time when differences between the sexes in attitudes, employment, and aptitudes are being progressively eroded, the statistics show that violent crimes and serial killings, particularly of victims selected at random, still remain almost exclusively a male preserve. Of course, murder in its wider sense is not limited to male criminals, but in general female killers tend to use different methods against different targets. They will frequently rely on poison to achieve their objectives rather than violence, and they will tend to target victims already close to them through work or family ties, crimes which tend to call for profiling on a much rarer basis.

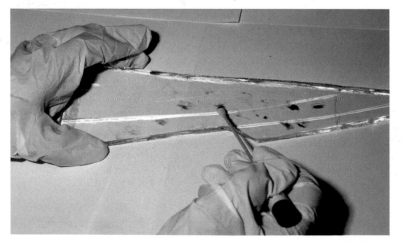

LEFT
An officer at a crime scene taking a swab of blood spots on a glass fragment, so that the swab can be subjected to DNA analysis.

ABOVE
A forensic scientist studying a DNA analysis in a specialist laboratory – this evidence was used to convict Peter Somers of the 1992 murder of Sarah Moslin in Yorkshire, England.

Finally, in an attempt to use modern profiling techniques to cast light on the most famous serial killer of the past, FBI profilers Roy Hazelwood and John Douglas took part in a U.S. television program in 1988 which set out to review the available evidence and determine which, in their opinion, of the seven likely suspects identified as Jack the Ripper by the TV production's researchers was the probable killer. The list included a journalist who had studied medicine and claimed to be a Satanist and who lived in Whitechapel, Dr Roslyn Donston, an emotionally troubled schoolteacher from a family of surgeons who committed suicide soon after the final murder, Montague John Druitt, royal physician Sir William Gull, Prince Albert Victor, grandson of Queen Victoria, and Aaron Kosminki, a deranged Polish Jew with an avowed hatred for women, who also lived in Whitechapel.

Other panelists on the program used various reasons for their choices. The profilers were convinced that, from the evidence of the crimes and the way in which they were committed, the killer was a white male in his middle to late twenties, of average intelligence, single and never married, who did not socialize with women, and who lived close to the crime scenes. If he had a job, it would be in menial work. He had probably been brought up in a broken home, where he might have been abused, and was very probably a loner, with poor personal hygiene and a disheveled appearance, who preferred a nocturnal lifestyle. Consequently he would not be able to approach his victims with any confidence, but needed to subdue them and kill them quickly.

All five of the program's experts chose Kosminski as the most likely identity for Jack the Ripper. In the case of the two profilers, he fitted their template so closely that John Douglas said afterwards that if Kosminski was not the killer, then someone very similar to him had been committing the crimes. Given the lack of any way of proving or disproving this allegation so long after the events, it remains a telling example of the power of profiling in helping to track down the infamous Jack's successors in the 21st century.

Profiling has proved to be an immensely valuable weapon in the fight against the violent criminal. In cases where forensic evidence like DNA samples, blood, hairs, and fingerprints are found at the scene of the crime but which do not throw up an immediate link to a suspect whose identity appears in police files, careful profiling can help to narrow down the search to produce a manageable number of suspects who can be tested for a match to the existing trace evidence. Where forensic evidence is lacking, details of the victim, the location and the scene of the crime, and other unmistakable pointers can help the profiler draw up a pattern of the person responsible, which can then be used to suggest other details of the offender's work, routine, lifestyle, home circumstances, and possible criminal record.

Profiling can help focus searches, avoid dead ends, and link crimes with relatively little evidence to others bearing the same offender signature where more evidence is available. It can help police to search in the right areas for their suspects, to manipulate the media to increase pressure on the criminal, and to question the suspect in the right way to persuade him to admit his guilt and confess to the crime. In all the case studies included in different chapters of this book, profiling is used in different ways to help solve different crimes. The common factor is the versatility of this increasingly powerful way of outwitting and isolating even the cleverest and deadliest of rapists, attackers, or serial killers, leaving them exposed and vulnerable at last to the forces of justice who seek to track them down.

ABOVE
A sample of human hair matted with blood found at a crime scene, kept in a clear plastic bag, and identified as potential evidence.

George Metesky

The Mad Bomber of New York

NOT ALL KILLERS meet their victims face to face. Where terrorism is involved, the violence — or sometimes, the threat of violence — is a means to an end. The crime is planned to extort a ransom, to pay off a real or imagined score against a person, an organization, or even a country, or simply to win the perpetrator a heady mix of fear and notoriety. In cases like these, the identity of the victim or victims is immaterial. Their intended fate simply serves the purpose of applying extra pressure on the authorities to give the criminal what he wants.

"One thing I can't understand is why the newspapers labeled me the Mad Bomber. That was unkind."

George Metesky on his arrest for placing 20 bombs in public places over a 17-year period, NY Journal-American January 22, 1957

In cases like these, the profiler would seem to have less direct information to work on. Yet in New York City in the late 1940s and early 1950s, Dr James Brussel was able to produce an astonishingly accurate profile of "The Mad Bomber of New York." This unseen assailant had succeeded in placing a succession of home-made bombs at different locations across the city over a period of sixteen years, without being identified or arrested. Apart from a series of cryptic notes, sometimes handwritten but often assembled from words cut from newspapers or magazines to avoid providing evidence, there was no lead which might enable the police to track down the criminal.

The early bombs had seemed trivial enough. The first was a simple pipe bomb, inside a wooden toolbox placed on a windowsill at the offices of the Consolidated Edison power company (always known to locals simply as

"Con Edison") on West 64th Street on November 16, 1940. The bomb failed to explode, and as it contained a note with the words "CON EDISON CROOKS, THIS IS FOR YOU," the police suspected it might have been intended merely as a threat, which had never been intended to explode, as this would have destroyed the message.

Fifteen months later, the police received a note from the bomber. The U.S. was now at war, and he announced that as a true patriot he would be suspending his bombing campaign while hostilities lasted, though he continued to leave anonymous messages for Con Edison, the police, different cinemas in the city, and even some individuals. But apart from another unexploded bomb found in the neighborhood of Con Edison's offices a year later, the next bomb was not found until March 29, 1950, when a third unexploded device was found in

Grand Central Station. Details showed it was almost certainly the work of the same hand, though it was considerably more professional.

Another bomb, planted in a phone box outside the New York Public Library *did* go off, though without any casualties, as did a second bomb at Grand Central Station. One after another bombs were being detonated all over the city, but the first one to cause casualties was hidden inside a cinema seat where it detonated at five minutes to eight in the evening of Saturday December 2, 1956 at the Paramount Movie Theater in Brooklyn. The cinema was crowded with early Christmas shoppers, so it was fortunate that no-one was killed by the blast — but eight people were injured, three of them seriously. By this time it was clear the Bomber was making the devices larger and larger, and it would only be a matter of time before innocent people would die. To make matters worse, he was goading the police with more and more provocative messages, mocking their inability to catch him.

So desperate were the police to find any means of narrowing down their search that Inspector Howard Finney asked a colleague, Captain James Cronin of the Missing Persons Bureau, if he could suggest any new way of tackling the case. Cronin recommended a criminal psychiatrist with a city practice named Dr. James Brussel, who might be able offer some advice as to the kind of person they should be looking for. The skeptical Finney

took his case notes to Brussel's office, and when the psychiatrist had finished studying the details of the case, his reply was truly staggering.

Brussel told the police the man they should be looking for was middle-aged, heavily built, and a foreign-born Roman Catholic. He was single, and probably paranoid. He had been loved by his mother to the point of obsession, though he had hated his father, and therefore lived with a brother or sister, probably in the nearby state of Connecticut. Furthermore, said Brussel, when they eventually caught him, the criminal would probably be wearing a double-breasted suit, and the chances were this would be buttoned up.

To the suspicious detectives, this seemed much too good to be true, a speculative leap in the dark which was little better than a random guess. But Dr Brussels' conclusions were based on careful, logical reasoning. First of all, he assumed the bomber was male, since this had invariably been the case with previous bomb outrages. It was clear from the placing of the bombs and the wording of the notes that the bomber had a deep grievance grudge against Con Edison, and could well be a former employee, who felt he had been wronged by the company, and was now looking for vengeance.

Other conclusions followed from the wording of the letters. His conviction that the world at large was against him pointed to paranoia, a condition which generally reaches its peak intensity around the age of 35, and if this had

triggered the start of his 16-year campaign, it would place him at around the age of 50. This conclusion was reinforced by the neatness of his printing, and the care taken in the assembly of the bombs, and his careful planning.

The language he used in the letters hinted at a writer whose native language was not English. He used archaic phrases like "dastardly deeds" and referred to "the Con Edison" rather than simply "Con Edison" as would a native New Yorker. Nevertheless, the language was grammatically correct and suggested a high school education as opposed to college. Among foreign-born ethnic groups in the United

States, the Slavs were most closely associated with the use of bombs as weapons, and the most likely religion was Roman Catholic.

Some of the letters had been posted from boxes in Westchester County, an area between New York City and the commuter towns of Connecticut. Many Slav immigrants lived in the area, so it was likely the bomber was based here too. Other clues in the evidence — principally the phallic shape of the bombs, the distorted letter "W" in the handwritten letters (which suggested the shape of a female breast), and the pattern of the cuts where the theater seats were slashed to hide the bombs — suggested to the psychiatrist the bomber was suffering from an Oedipus complex. Most patients with this condition tended to dislike their fathers, had probably lost their mother when young, and lived with a single relative. A double-breasted suit was popular in the fashions of the time, but for someone afflicted with this combination of conditions, buttoning up the suit would be a subconscious safeguard against a hostile and threatening world.

The profile was astonishingly detailed, but still failed to offer the police what they most needed — a lead to a possible suspect. Then Dr. Brussel suggested they use the profile as a direct trap to catch the person it fitted. He suggested the police release the information to the media. Because the police had banned the bomber's earlier letters from being published, he had been growing more and more angry at being starved of publicity, and Dr.

Brussel was convinced this final outrage would cause him to reveal himself.

At first, as the police feared, there was a succession of false leads. Only when the bomber finally telephoned Dr. Brussel direct did he realize his prediction had been completely correct. There was still no way of knowing the bomber's name and address, but the police were now searching through the records of all the companies which had been absorbed into the Con Edison group, looking for details of injured employees. At last, they found a reference to one George Metesky of number 17, 4th Street, Waterbury, Connecticut. He had suffered an accident on the same date as the bomber had revealed in one of his letters. He had been working for the United Electric & Power Company which had been taken over by Con Edison, but his claim that he had contracted tuberculosis as a result of the accident had been turned down by the company, and Metesky had written a number of angry letters. In one of them he had threatened the company, promising retribution for what he called its "dastardly deeds."

The police called at Metesky's home to arrest him, where they found him wearing a dressing-gown. He was asked to change into outdoor clothes, whereupon he dressed in a double-breasted suit, which he buttoned up before emerging. He was tried and found guilty but insane, and was confined to a criminal asylum until his release in 1973. He returned to live with his family in the Waterbury house and died in 1994 at the age of 90.

TOP
The Main Branch of the New York Public Library on Fifth Avenue, between 40th and 42nd Streets, where one of Metesky's bombs detonated in a public telephone booth.

LEFT
Grand Central Station, where another of the "Mad Bomber's" devices went off, though without causing any casualties.

CHAPTER ONE:
WHAT IS PROFILING?

1: What is profiling?

CLEARLY BY THE 1970S, criminal profiling was beginning to prove a useful and effective technique to help reduce the suspect pool in a complex criminal investigation, especially in cases where other factors such as motive, family relationships, witness sightings, or forensic evidence to limit the number of potential suspects were not apparent in the initial stages of the investigation. This makes it possible for the investigators to concentrate and prioritize their investigation, reducing the time wasted in exploring areas which prove to be of less relevance in solving the crime. In cases of serial crimes, profiling has also been used to help establish which crimes were the work of a single offender by identifying crime scene indicators unique to that criminal, and by looking for similarities in behavior patterns as shown by the evidence in different cases.

Because profiling involves the study of the psychology of the criminal involved, it also makes it possible for the investigators to assess the potential for a nuisance criminal involved in relatively less serious offences to escalate to more dangerous or more violent crimes. Even when the criminal is finally identified and caught, the work of the profilers can be vital in suggesting to the police officers involved in the investigation the best way for them to approach the interrogation of their suspect, to ensure the evidence they need is obtained as quickly, economically, and effectively as possible.

So how does profiling work? The idea that a criminal's personality is revealed in the type of crime committed, the methods by which it was carried out, and the signs found at the scene of the crime itself is fundamental to profiling. This means that profiling will generally be most effective in cases where the police have little information to help them solve the case using traditional methods, and may well be unsure as to the type of individual — in terms of age, background, experience, work, or other identifiable characteristics — they should begin looking for.

In addition, the more violent crimes like rape or murder are frequently the subject of profiles because they tend to reveal more signs which reveal aspects of the perpetrator's personality at the crime scene than other, less violent criminal acts such as burglary and petty theft. Consequently the more violent crimes are more susceptible to profiling, and with the increasing likelihood of repeat offences, they represent particularly urgent priorities for the investigators involved.

Influences on personality

Psychology tells us that each individual personality is formed by a range of different influences. These include:

• inherited factors from biological parents, grandparents,
  or more distant antecedents
• cultural factors in an individual's upbringing
• the environment in which the individual grew up or
  currently lives
• the experiences they undergo in their lives

Criminals who show violence in the crimes they commit have markedly different personalities from those of the law-abiding majority. Profilers assume that these sharp differences in attitude and thinking are reflected in the crime scenes. Furthermore, each violent criminal will have personality differences which separate them from other types of violent criminal, and these differences will also be reflected in the evidence found at the scenes of the crimes they commit.

In a murder case, for example, the manner in which the victim was killed is of vital importance to the profiler. On the other hand, more subtle signs can be equally useful in narrowing down

ABOVE
Violence at an early age, as in this teenage fight, often sows the seeds for future criminality of a much darker nature.

the profile of the perpetrator. For example, a neat and carefully arranged crime scene suggests an "organized" killer, whereas one which is chaotic points to a more "disorganized" type of personality. These two types are explained in greater detail in Chapter 4.

An additional result of this linking of personality to the method of committing a crime and the evidence found at the scene is that these will tend to remain relatively unchanged for an individual criminal. These "signature" elements — the criminal's calling card that he leaves at each crime scene — can be all-important to the criminal, who may well go to great lengths to ensure that a certain ritual, however bizarre, is performed identically at each crime scene, even where this is handing the police additional evidence which could well help to unmask him in the end.

In one series of crimes in the Mid-West, two elderly women were murdered and their corpses were left in full view, in a public park. Neither had been raped, but in both cases the car keys and driver's licenses of the victims were placed on their stomachs. Then the body of another murder victim in a state several hundred miles away was laid out in the same unusual way, with driver's license and car keys laid carefully on the stomach.

In one sense this might have appeared to be the work of a different killer, because of the geographical separation and because this was a completely different type of victim. In this case, the murderer had killed a young man working as a female impersonator rather than an elderly woman. Nonetheless, the signature element in both cases was so strong that police concluded that the same killer had committed all three crimes, and only realized the third victim was actually male after carrying out the attack.

A Genetic Answer?

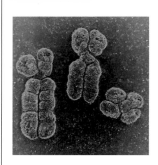

Human chromosomes contain the DNA that provides the instructions for the growth, development, and functioning of the organism. If deciphering the code for human life does indeed lead to a better understanding of the function of every gene in our body, as modern science believes, will it eventually be possible to predict who will develop heart disease, violent tendencies, or other characteristics of human nature?

Scientists the world over believe that genes do play an important part in the making of our behavioral and medical attributes but that these are due at least as much to environmental influences as they are to genetic influences.

ABOVE
Picture of human chromosomes, magnified more than 6,000 times on a scanning electron microscope.

RIGHT
Assistants at the Forensic Science Service laboratories in south London, England, extracting DNA from samples collected at crime scenes. Identification of criminals was to be made easier by adding samples from the DNA of 13,000 prisoners and mentally disordered offenders to the U.K. police database.

Changing patterns of violence

On the other hand, some things *will* change. Very often violent criminals become completely addicted to the violence they wreak on their helpless victims. The violence may well cease to be the means to an end, in terms of committing a robbery or a rape, and become so enjoyable to the criminal that it becomes the main objective of the crime. This means that the scenes of successive crimes committed by the same criminal show marked similarities in terms of the choice of victim and the method of operating (modus operandi), but a steadily increasing progression in terms of the level of violence involved.

Serial criminals change in other ways too. Psychological studies have shown that many seriously disturbed and violent criminals do in fact have IQs which are higher than average. This means they are often able to learn from their experiences and refine their methods of operation — provided these still fulfill their psychological needs — to make it less likely that their victim

LEFT
A classic example of the disorder of a chaotic crime scene in St. Petersburg in Russia – "Murder Capital of Europe" with an annual toll of 650 victims – where homicide detectives search the apartment of an unidentified woman whose dismembered body was found in a garbage container.

will escape or that they will be caught when committing their crime. Clearly this imposes another burden on the investigators, since they have a much better chance of catching a serial criminal at a relatively early stage in his or her career, before they learn from any initial mistakes and refine their routine for finding and attacking a victim to make their apprehension less likely.

Profiling doesn't set out to explain the reasons why a particular type of criminal may have developed in the way that he or she did. Academic experts in psychology are still at odds over the relative importance of genetic inheritance or upbringing in forming personality traits — the classic nature versus nurture debate. What profilers do instead is assume that the differences between criminals and the law-abiding citizens, and between different types of criminals, can be read by careful studies of each crime or series of crimes, and these can be used to shed light on the offender's personality without any attempt to explain how and why the criminal became the person capable of committing the crimes.

Profiling — an art or a science?

Some profilers describe the subject as a science, with clear and reliable links between different items of evidence and the personality of the criminal involved. Others describe it as an art, since many specific signs may appear to point in different directions, reflecting the infinite variations possible between different individual criminal personalities, and which force the profiler to draw the right balance between these conflicting signals. Almost certainly both viewpoints are right, and successful profiling remains a combination of the two.

Profiling also depends on two different techniques — inductive profiling and deductive profiling — to deliver results. Inductive profiling makes the basic assumption that where crimes which are committed by different people show basic similarities in "modus operandi," or method, and signature, then the criminals responsible must show personality traits in common. This is a relatively simple technique, since it links personality with crime scene evidence in a straightforward way, and makes use of information from past crimes and their known offenders. This knowledge is used to make an assessment based on the links shown by similar crime scenes in the past.

Deductive profiling is a more complex procedure, since it involves using the crime scene evidence to open a window into the mind of the criminal involved. It also draws upon other essential evidence like full details of the victims involved, and therefore takes much longer to produce a finished profile than

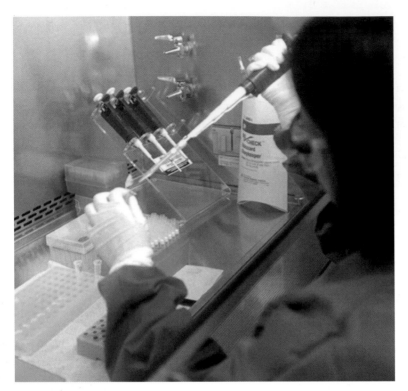

LEFT
A technician prepares to isolate DNA from crime scene samples at the new crime laboratory in Syracuse, New York.

inductive profiling. In most cases, the finished profile uses a combination of these techniques: inductive profiling to point to the basic type of criminal personality involved, and deductive profiling to reveal the traits of the individual criminal against the more general conclusions of the type to which he belongs.

Finally, it remains important to remember some of the limitations of profiling. By its very nature, it can never lead police to an individual criminal. All it can do is point them in the right direction to help their investigations bear fruit. Profiling can be of especial assistance to police when they have no suspect or when the pool of possible suspects is so large that it would benefit a more detailed and specific analysis. In some types of crime like burglary, assault, or even a single murder with a particular individual or motive in mind, however, it is very unlikely to work at all because either there is insufficient information on which to construct a profile or the identity of the principal suspect is clear from the beginning, and even in cases where profiling could help, it doesn't always produce results.

This in itself has caused some controversy between profilers and policemen. Those police officers who tend to rely on their own personal experience from possibly hundreds of successful cases may well discount the usefulness of profiling because of its apparently vague suggestions. They expect the method to provide hard facts, which it is simply not able to do. On the other hand, faced with professional reluctance to value their efforts properly, some profilers have made exaggerated claims for the usefulness of their work in making it possible to catch violent criminals.

In the early 1990s, the FBI carried out a research study into the effectiveness of its profilers' efforts. This covered a total of 192 cases where profilers had been called in to give advice. In all those cases, a total of 88, or some 46%, were actually solved. However, when the results were examined in more detail, it was found that profiling only helped to identify a subject in just 17% of these cases.

Nevertheless, it remains equally important to remember that this does not prove that profiling is in any sense a failure. Given that profiling is only involved in cases where traditional investigation methods are not working quickly enough, even this kind of success rate is remarkable. Were it not for profiling, it is at least possible that none of these cases would have been solved at all, and many more people would have fallen victims to the killers or rapists involved. The other important factor is that many of the cases studied related to the earlier days of profiling, and that the whole process involves learning from experience, so that the effectiveness of the technique is improving all the time.

BELOW
FBI agents check out the crime scene at an Exxon service station in Fredericksburg, Virginia, where Kenneth Bridges had become the eighth victim of the Washington Sniper on October 11 2002.

Arthur Shawcross

Interrupted Development

SOMETIMES, other apparently misleading results in a profile can be explained by factors of which the profilers were unaware at the time, and can actually reinforce the accuracy of the profile when they become known. In the case of a series of murders of prostitutes in upstate New York in 1988 and 1989, police seemed to have no clear leads to help them isolate a suspect. The modus operandi was simple and consistent. The killer would pick up a prostitute close to the town of Rochester, New York, take her to a secluded spot for sex, would kill her by strangulation or a heavy blow, and then drop the corpse in a nearby river. On several occasions the bodies were found with the genital area cut away and it was believed the killer had removed the body parts as trophies or for cannibalism.

By the end of 1989 a total of ten bodies had been found, and FBI profiler Gregg McCrary was called in to suggest a means of finding and trapping the killer. He suggested to the police that the criminal they were looking for was aged in his late 20s to possibly 30 years old, basing these conclusions on the age of the victims, most of whom had been in their 20s or 30s. He was clearly mobile, since the women had entered his car when picked up, and he was plausible enough for them to have trusted him as a potential client. He also suggested the criminal would be confident enough to hang

TOP RIGHT
Police helicopters fitted with a forward looking infra-red camera speeded up Shawcross' capture after one spotted him leaving a crime scene.

LEFT
Shawcross leaves court after pleading guilty to a charge of second degree murder.

FAR RIGHT
Home to a killer: the block at 241 Alexander Street, Rochester NY, where Shawcross and his wife shared an apartment

BELOW: LEFT TO RIGHT
Shawcross' victims – Patricia Ives, Frances Brown, June Cicero, Darlene Trippi, Anna Maria Steffen, Dorothy Blackburn, June Stotts, Maria Welch, Elizabeth Gibson (thought to be one of his victims), and Dorothy Keeler. All except Keeler were aged between 22-34, which helped profilers suggest a likely age for their attacker.

around places where police officers could be found off duty, and might even question them about the progress of the investigations. McCrary also suggested that he would return to the bodies of his recent victims to carry out further mutilations, which might provide a means of catching him.

Yet when police finally trapped the killer, it appeared the profile had been misleading in one respect at least. The police had been acting on the suggestion of trapping the suspect in the act of mutilating one of the victims' bodies and had been flying helicopter patrols along the local waterways. In January 1990 a police helicopter crew spotted a woman's body in frozen Salmon Creek. On a bridge overlooking the creek they saw an overweight middle-aged man climbing into a car and driving off. A patrol car was alerted, which tailed him to a nearby nursing home, where he was arrested and taken in for questioning.

On the face of it, he was an unpromising prospect as the potential killer. His name was Arthur Shawcross, he was married but enjoying a relationship with a woman working at the nursing home. He was also 45 years old,

considerably older than the profile had suggested. Furthermore, he didn't own a car, but was a familiar figure traveling around the local area by bicycle. The car belonged to his woman friend, and the police were forced to let him go for lack of evidence, though they held on to the car for a more thorough examination.

However, when they checked their records, they realized Arthur Shawcross was a much more promising suspect than first appeared. Seventeen years earlier he had been sentenced to 25 years in prison for murdering and mutilating two young children in the New York community of Watertown. While in prison he had managed to behave as a model prisoner and convince the parole board that he no longer represented a threat, and so he was released after serving 15 years of his sentence, on condition that he kept away from anywhere where young children could be found.

As a paroled child killer, he had been compelled to move from one community to another after campaigns had been started by local parents to alert the authorities to the danger he presented to their children. Finally he had settled in Rochester a year before, where he

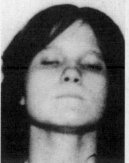

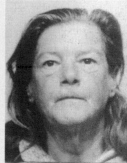

had married, begun working at nights preparing salads for a local food distribution company, and spent his days fishing. He also used his girlfriend's car on numerous occasions, and spent a lot of his time talking to off-duty policemen at the local Dunkin' Donut fast-food café about the killings and the investigation. Finally, when the car was thoroughly searched, the investigators found an earring from one of the missing women.

Questioned by police about the evidence found in the car, Shawcross finally confessed to the police that he had been responsible for the killings, though in each case he blamed his anger on the fact that the women had taunted him or tried to rob him. He also revealed that after the first killing, he had watched for any signs of a search for the missing woman. In view of what seemed public indifference to her death, Shawcross seemed to realize she represented another vulnerable group of potential victims and one which, given his history, was much easier for him to approach than young children.

Why had he carried out the killings? When taken for trial for the murders of ten known victims and another to which Shawcross had also confessed, his defense team brought in experts to claim he was suffering from post-traumatic stress disorder after childhood abuse and war service in Vietnam. The prosecution also retained a psychiatrist, who was advised by FBI profiler Bob Ressler that Shawcross' war records showed he was a malingerer rather than a brave and dedicated soldier, and that consequently his evidence was untrustworthy.

In the end even the defense psychiatrist realized Shawcross had been lying to her even when pretending to be under hypnosis, and the jury found him guilty of all 11 murders. He was sentenced to spend the rest of his life in prison, this time with no possibility of parole. And the discrepancy in the profile on the question of his age? Because he had spent 15 years in prison, this had delayed his criminal development by the same amount. In terms of the progression of his violence, he was still effectively 30 years old, the age predicted by the FBI profiler.

BELOW
Medical examiner Dr. Nicholas Forbes testifying at the Shawcross trial using an overhead projection of a patient's injury chart to describe the injuries inflicted on June Stotts.

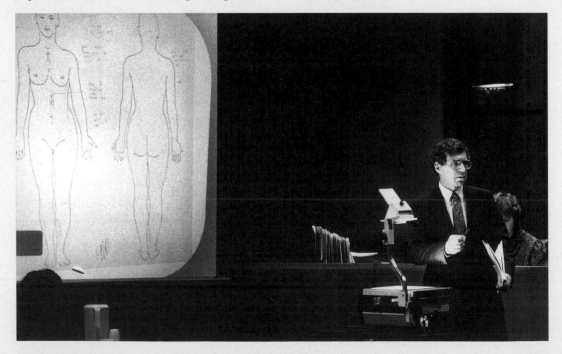

2: Different ways to prepare a profile

PROFILERS COMMONLY FOLLOW a routine in considering the evidence they are presented with in relation to a particular crime, or series of crimes. However, profilers in different areas or different countries often follow slightly different approaches to reach the same final objectives. For example, the main systems followed by U.S. and U.K. profilers include the Crime Scene Analysis routine pioneered and taught by the FBI, and the similar technique of Investigative Psychology as developed by the British profiler Professor David Canter.

The techniques taught in the FBI's Crime Scene Analysis program developed in the early 1980s, for example, include six progressive steps which make up the profiling process. The first, **Profiling Inputs**, involves collecting and assessing the evidence

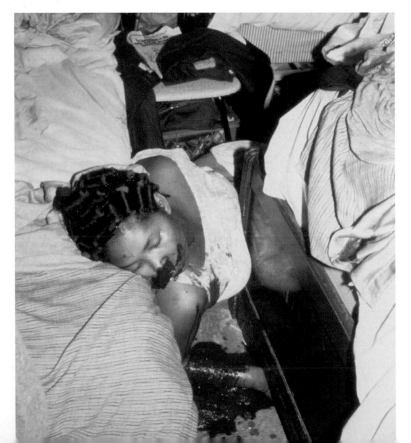

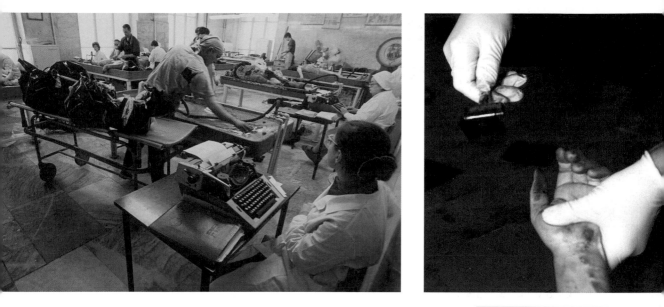

relating to the case being profiled. In practice, this would include any photographs which may have been taken to show the victim and the wider context of the crime scene, the results of any autopsy of the victim, and any other forensic information needed to establish what happened before, during, and after the crime as clearly and precisely as possible. This stage is seen as particularly important, since the detail and accuracy of the information on which the profile is based will effectively limit the detail and accuracy of the resulting profile.

The second stage, **Decision Process Models**, involves arranging and classifying all the information collected in the first stage into a logical pattern, to establish the basic facts about the crime. This might include deciding how many victims were involved, for example, and whether the crime was one of a series carried out by an individual criminal.

Next, **Crime Assessment** involves the profiler reconstructing the sequence of events which make up the crime, and studying the specific behavior of both the criminal and the victim. The purpose of this stage is to help the profiler understand the role of each individual in the crime, and to use that information in developing the resulting criminal profile.

The **Criminal Profile** which follows these preliminary stages is made up of a list of background, physical, and behavioral characteristics the criminal is likely to possess. The FBI system also includes the drawing up of advice at this stage on how the investigators can best approach the tasks of identifying and catching the perpetrator. The **Investigation** stage covers the use of the actual profile in the investigation program, and if at this

ABOVE LEFT
Victims give up their secrets – a series of post-mortems being carried out on corpses in Moscow, Russia's capital.

ABOVE
Forensic scientist in St. Petersburg taking samples from the bloody hand of a corpse.

stage no subjects are produced, or if new evidence emerges which appears to contradict the initial profile based on the previously existing evidence, then the profile is re-examined and modified to take these factors into account.

The final stage of the process, the **Apprehension**, may or may not take place, depending on the success of the investigation in tracking down and arresting the perpetrator of the crime. Even in cases where the profile is accurate, the criminal responsible may have been arrested by another authority, may have been arrested on a completely different charge, or may simply have given up committing crimes, in the shorter term at least. However, where the criminal has been caught, the Apprehension stage involves cross-checking the details of the profile with the characteristics of the actual offender to determine how accurate it was, and to use the information to help with future profiles of similar crimes.

Investigative Psychology

Much like the FBI's Crime Scene Analysis routine, Canter's Investigative Psychology makes use of background statistics relating to a database of different criminal populations. This means drawing up the characteristics of known types of criminal groups, in terms of the types of crime they commit. When a new crime of that type occurs, the unknown criminal can be compared to that criminal grouping, to produce a list of the characteristics the unknown criminal is likely to possess.

Investigative Psychology began in 1985 when David Canter, then teaching psychology students at the University of Surrey in southern England, was asked to explore the possibilities of using his psychological expertise to help Scotland Yard, the headquarters of the London Metropolitan Police Force, with criminal investigations. The first case involved was a series of attacks and murders committed by a criminal known only by his nickname, the Railway Rapist (*see* Case Study 4, page 42). As a result of experience on these

BELOW
One of the cleverest and most prolific of serial killers, Ted Bundy, invariably chose his young female victims according to a clear physical type, thought to be similar to his former girlfriend. This is a TV still from his final interview with Dr. James Dobson the night before his execution.

cases, the technique of Investigative Psychology was developed into a University teaching program, first at Surrey and then at the University of Liverpool. The technique involves a series of steps, like the FBI approach, but based on considering five different aspects of the interaction between the criminal and his victim, rather than following a set of chronological steps in the production of the profile.

The first, **Interpersonal Coherence**, is based on the assumption that criminals will deal with other people in their ordinary daily lives in similar ways to those with which they deal with their victims. As an extension of this, the victims may themselves be linked with people of particular importance in the background of the criminal, much as the U.S. serial killer Ted Bundy was believed to select those victims who most closely resembled his former girlfriend.

Secondly, the **Significance of Time and Place**, looks at the time and location of the crime and considers what light these may throw on how criminals views their surroundings and their own timetable. For example the time of an attack may suggest the criminal's work schedule or his activities. The location may provide a guide to information about the mobility of criminals, and how they select and reach the location of the crime.

The third factor concerns **Criminal Characteristics**. This involves classifying the criminal responsible for a given crime into the right criminal group, so that the likely characteristics of criminals in that group can be included in the profile drawn up for the investigators of that crime.

The fourth aspect, **Criminal Career**, involves making an assessment of whether the criminal has an existing record, and what kind of crimes are most likely to have been involved. For example, a crime where the perpetrator has shown a degree of skill in breaking into the victim's house undetected might suggest an earlier career as a burglar.

Finally, **Forensic Awareness** relates to evidence at the crime scene which may show whether or not the criminal has any knowledge or awareness of the routines and techniques involved when the police collect evidence, and the types of evidence collected. At its simplest, forensic awareness might involve wearing gloves to avoid leaving fingerprints, but in rape cases the use of a condom or more particularly, washing the victim's body to remove traces of bodily fluids containing DNA, may suggest that the criminal has carried out rapes previously. Information like this can be helpful to the police, in narrowing down a large number of potential suspects, to focus their attention on the most promising candidates.

David Carpenter

The Trailside Killer

NOT ALL PROFILING helps to net the potential killer at the first attempt. Sometimes the availability of more information makes it possible to remedy incorrect assumptions or to add additional detail which may finally succeed in pointing the way to the person responsible for a series of violent crimes. In the case of the so-called "Trailside Killer" in California, the first victim was discovered in August 1979. Edda Kane, a married 44-year-old bank manager went missing while hiking up Mount Tamalpais, overlooking the Golden Gate and the Bay of San Francisco. Searchers found her naked body in a kneeling position. She had been killed by a single shot to the head, and there was no sign of sexual assault, and cash and credit cards were missing.

The killer struck again seven months later in March 1980, and again in park territory. Once again the victim had been stripped and left in a kneeling position, but this time the cause of death was repeated stab wounds to the chest. Disturbingly, seven months after that a third victim was found, though this time she was lying on her back, fully clothed, with a fatal gunshot wound to the right side of her head. By this time the police had found a suspect, one

Mark McDermand, whose mother and mentally ill brother had been found shot in their cabin on the mountain. Detectives found he possessed several firearms, but though he confessed to murdering his brother and mother, none of his weapons matched those used in two of the three Trailside Murders up to that time.

News went from bad to worse for the investigators. A month later, in November 1980, another young woman went missing when hiking the park trails. Her body was found a day later, lying in a shallow grave next to that of yet another woman who had gone missing a month before, both of them killed by gunshots. To the horror of detectives two more bodies, those of a couple who had also gone missing in the park the previous month were found, by grim coincidence, later that same day.

Witnesses who reported people behaving suspiciously in the park produced a bewildering variety of descriptions. The only piece of solid evidence seemed to be a pair of bifocal spectacles at the site of the second murder which may well have belonged to the killer, and which were found to be standard prison issue. A local psychologist was brought in for advice, and he suggested the criminal was probably

ABOVE
San Francisco's Golden Gate Bridge, overlooked by Mount Tamalpais where the Trailside Killer's first victim was found naked, kneeling, and shot through the head.

ABOVE
Most of his victims were those of single white female hikers, attacked and murdered while walking California's parkland trails.

good-looking, with a winning and persuasive personality, who was likely to take souvenirs from his victims, and who was likely to continue killing. He recommended the police continued to follow any potential suspects, in the hope they would be led to where the evidence might be kept.

Police also mounted a series of traps, with female officers posing as hikers and climbers, but nothing positive resulted. By now the FBI's own profilers had studied information published on the case, and they had noticed that all the attacks had taken place in heavily wooded areas, at least a mile from any public road. The only partial exception was the second victim whose body lay quite close to a service road used by park staff, which would not have been familiar to the general public. These two facts suggested that the killer was a local man who knew the area well.

The method by which the killer had attacked his victims, by sneaking up on them from behind and shooting or stabbing them in a blitz attack, suggested to the FBI that he was far less likely to be a good-looking, persuasive individual. In their view, he was almost certainly a withdrawn loner who lacked the conversational skill to approach these fit young women and overcome them without the advantage of surprise. Because the victims showed a wide range of ages and types, there was no evidence of selection, though the secluded locations of the crimes suggested the killer waited there for any potential victim to arrive in his clutches.

The profilers went further. They suggested he had spent time in prison for other crimes. All the victims were white, which suggested the killer was white too. They estimated his age as low to mid-thirties and considered he was probably working in a non-managerial mechanical or industrial role, though he had shown enough intelligence to avoid the police so far. Other classic symptoms of this type of killer included arson, cruelty to animals, and even childhood bed-wetting, and profiler John Douglas suggested he might even suffer from a speech impediment – because of his deliberate avoidance of locations where he might meet people in greater numbers than one at a time, and because overcoming and killing healthy young women might be his way of making up

FBI profiler John Douglas, who profiled the Trailside Killer and who correctly identified him as white, with a speech impediment, and a history of both childhood bed-wetting and cruelty to animals.

for his handicap. Alternatively, reasoned Douglas, his problem could be bad acne or other facial disfigurement – but any more serious physical disability would probably limit his ability to overcome his victims.

Next, on March 29, 1981 the killer shot a couple in another local park near Santa Cruz. This time, though the woman died her partner survived and he was able to describe a man with teeth which were crooked and yellowed, though he estimated he was in his fifties. Other witnesses, when given this description, linked it to a red, nearly new, European car, and in the meantime the ballistics evidence showed this was indeed the Trailside Killer.

Finally, another young woman went missing on May 1. This time her family and friends revealed she had arranged to meet a 50-year-old teacher at her printing college, one David Carpenter, who drove a red Fiat. Other witnesses helped tie Carpenter to additional attacks in the area, and he was finally arrested for the Trailside murders.

Police found that Carpenter was indeed above average intelligence, and had a history of both childhood bed-wetting and cruelty to animals. He had continually been picked on because of a severe stutter and had served time in prison for attacking a woman partner with a knife and hammer. The only reason he had evaded detection for so long was that his different crimes had fallen into the territory of different police forces, which made the search much more complicated than it would otherwise have been.

John Duffy

The Railway Rapist

DURING THE EARLY 1980S, a series of rapes was committed across a wide sweep of the outer suburbs of London. Police were actively searching for the criminal responsible when it became clear that the perpetrator was escalating from rape to murder. Three of his later victims were killed after being raped, with the criminal using a tourniquet to strangle them. In all three cases, the bodies were dumped close to railway lines, and it was clear that the earlier attacks took place close to different parts of the railway network. As a result, the unknown criminal was tagged the "Railway Rapist" and a massive police manhunt was launched.

Professor David Canter of the University of Sussex, in southern England, was asked to help the investigation by drawing up a profile of the kind of person the police should be looking for. After examining the huge quantities of information generated by the police operation up to that point, he was able to reach a series of conclusions about the person responsible. He assumed that the attacker lived in the area outlined by the locations of the first three known rapes, in the Kilburn area of north-west London. Because there was a gap in the earlier attacks between October 24, 1982 and January 1984, Canter suggested the criminal might well have been arrested and imprisoned for some unrelated offence, possibly something involving aggressive behavior,

ABOVE
Railway Rapist John Duffy, found guilty of three murders and eight rapes, carried out his attacks close to the local railway network and dumped the bodies of his victims close to the tracks.

perhaps under the influence of alcohol.

Based on the evidence from the crime scenes and evidence supplied by the women who had survived their attacks, he was also able to suggest the attacker was about five feet nine inches tall, right-handed, fair-haired and aged between 25 and 30. Certain details of the crimes showed the offender was sexually experienced, and traces of bodily fluids found at the scenes of the crimes showed his blood group was A, and he was a secretor. In other words, his blood group was apparent from other body fluids like tears, sweat, saliva, or semen. In other ways, it was clear he was familiar with some of the types of evidence the police would look for. He would try to wipe off evidence of the rapes from his victims' bodies, and in the case of the murders the police found the pubic areas had been burned, again to eliminate potential evidence.

Canter also assumed that the attacker had been living with a wife or girlfriend, though probably with no children. This related to evidence which showed he was able to approach his victims confidently enough to ask directions without immediately frightening them off, which suggested a confidence with women which would probably have come from a stable relationship. On the other hand, one of the women he had killed had been a 15-year-old named Maartje Tamboezer. Canter concluded the attacker was not likely to have had children

LEFT
15-year-old Maartje Tamboezer was one of the women raped and murdered by the attacker, which led profilers to assume the criminal had no children of his own, otherwise her age would almost certainly have been an inhibiting factor.

BOTTOM
Hackney Wick st[...] East London, En[...] where the body [...] Duffy's murder v[...] was found.

of his own, since this would have inhibite[...] from carrying out a violent attack on som[...] still a child herself.

He suggested it was likely the criminal [...] worked in a semi-casual skilled or semi-s[...] job, which would not tend to bring him i[...] close contact with the public, but which v[...] allow him time off during the working we[...] He was also likely to be something of a "l[...] with perhaps one or two reasonably close [...] friends, but little contact with women, especially at work, which might account for the level of anger he displayed towards his female victims. However, the use of a tourniquet to strangle his victims was an unusual feature which did not link to any particular conclusion.

Provided with the profile, the police were able to re-examine their pool of 2,000 potential subjects. Almost immediately they became aware

of the 1,505th person on their list, one John Patrick Duffy, who had been arrested for raping his ex-wife after she had left him. Not only was he one of the very few suspects who lived in the Kilburn area, but he also fitted many of the other factors included in the profile. He worked as a railway carpenter, which would account for his relative freedom during working hours, and his clear knowledge of the railway system. In addition, use of a tourniquet to stop the flow of blood would be standard first-aid procedure for many serious accidents involving the use of sharp carpenters' tools.

Duffy was shorter than Canter's profile suggested, but this turned out to be because several surviving victims had made the common mistake of over-estimating the height of such a threatening and aggressive figure. The police decided to keep a close watch on their suspect, and his conduct raised enough suspicion for him to be arrested. Forensic examination revealed that fibers found on his victims' bodies were identical with those on Duffy's clothing, and an unusual type of string used to tie them up was found at his home. Surviving victims picked him out at identity parades and in 1988 he was put on trial and found guilty of both rapes and murders and jailed for life, without possibility of parole.

Later, several other facts came to light to explain Duffy's actions. Though the locations of his attacks spread out to cover an area of outer London some 100 miles across, it was clear that all the sites were close to railway tracks, and all were also close to places he knew from visiting friends or relatives, or from his leisure activities. At the time when his attacks changed from rapes to murders, police found he had seen one of his earlier victims when he had attended court for the attacks on his wife. The woman had taken a close look at him but clearly failed to recognize him. Nonetheless, Duffy had probably decided no future victim should be able to identify him, and from then on he killed all the women he attacked.

An additional complication was the presence of an accomplice in the earliest rapes. David Mulcahy, a boyhood friend of Duffy, was the reason why some of the evidence given by victims of these crimes in giving descriptions seemed confusing at first. As a result of later questioning of Duffy in prison, he admitted to 17 additional rapes and the one murder for which he had not been previously convicted. He also identified Mulcahy as his helper. Mulcahy was arrested and charged in 1999 with taking part in several of the rapes and one of the murders, and also sentenced to life imprisonment.

LEFT
Anne Lock, one of the victims murdered by Duffy and Mulcahy.

TOP LEFT
Police mugshot of David Mulcahy, charged with rape and murder in 1999, as the accomplice of John Duffy.

CHAPTER THREE:
AT THE SCENE...

3: At the scene...

I N MANY CASES, the first step in producing a profile is to carry out a careful study of the crime scene, either directly at the crime scene as soon as possible after the crime has been discovered, or indirectly, once the crime scene has been cleared and all the evidence and records gathered at the time of the original investigation are available for the profiler to examine. Although the process of collecting information will already have been carried out by the detectives investigating the crime, the profiler's aim is to draw out a different type of information, above and beyond the physical evidence uncovered. Some profilers go further, and emphasize that their first step is actually to concentrate on those factors which reveal the type of person who carried out the crime, in preference to the conventional forensic evidence which will confirm the identity of that individual once he or she has been identified and arrested.

What does that mean in practice? Instead of looking for concrete evidence such as individual splashes of blood, fingerprints, or footprints, the profiler will look first and foremost for signs which throw light on the kind of person who committed the crime, in other words, the profiler's aim is to try to understand the psychological make-up of the offender. To the experienced profiler, the scene of a murder can reveal whether the criminal is a disorganized, asocial offender who may be of below-average intelligence, or cleverer and much more organized individual who carries out the murder in a very different way.

For example, in the case of a triple murder in Warwick, Rhode Island, in September 1989, profiler Gregg McCrary identified a series of signals which helped direct the search for the killer. The victims were 39-year-old Joan Heaton and her two daughters, ten-year-old Jennifer and eight-year-old Melissa. Between them, the three

had suffered a total of more than 120 slash and stab wounds, delivered in a frenzied attack using a knife which had been taken from their kitchen. The bodies of the mother and older daughter had been found in the hallway, partly covered by blood-soaked blankets, and with a teddy bear and a doll placed at Jennifer's feet. Melissa was found in the kitchen, where it seemed likely she had been trying to reach the phone, to call for help.

The fact that the criminal had found the murder weapon in the house rather than bringing it with him suggested a disorganized killer. The toys placed at the feet of one of his victims suggested he knew them reasonably well before the attack. The height of the window through which he had been able to break into the house suggested he was reasonably athletic. Finally, no-one questioned by police in the area remembered seeing any strangers at the time of the killings.

All these signals pointed to someone who lived close to the scene of the murders. The neighborhood was predominantly white, Irish, and Roman Catholic, so this meant it was possible the killer had a similar background. However, Gregg McCrary was able to produce a more precise pointer. The sheer frenzy of the attacks suggested the killer might well have cut himself. For this reason, McCrary urged the investigators to look out for a local man with a criminal record who had recently cut himself, and also to check samples of all the blood at the scene, since some of it might belong to the perpetrator.

Craig Price was a local man who matched the profile in all respects except one. He had a cut on his hand, which he explained had resulted from punching through a car window while trying to commit a robbery. When the police checked, they found no-one had reported a break-in to a car, and there were no fragments of automobile glass at the place he claimed the robbery attempt had taken place. Though he had a record of petty crime, he had never before made an admission of guilt. More remarkably, he was black in this largely white neighborhood, but because he had been brought up in the area, with many white friends, he had not been seen as a stranger by local witnesses. When questioned by police, he finally admitted to the three murders. Though profiling had helped to lead the police to their suspect, his guilt was finally confirmed by classic forensic evidence — his DNA was found in the blood samples retrieved from the scene, and his palm print was found at the point where he had entered the house.

Distinctions between the psychological makeup of killers will be reflected at the crime scene in terms of factors like the danger of discovery of the location and the amount of physical evidence

ABOVE
U.S. President John F. Kennedy is killed by the shots fired by assassin Lee Harvey Oswald in Dallas, November 1963, in a classic crime of emotional intent.

found. If the crime scene is within public access and the physical evidence uncovered is poorly concealed or even left behind, this hints at a disorganized criminal. The organized criminal, on the other hand, will make sure that as much evidence as possible is destroyed. The location of the crime will be planned and researched to make the chance of discovery minimal, and the body may even be taken away and disposed of elsewhere, to confuse the authorities and reduce the risk of being tracked down. These preliminary findings go some way to decoding what type of person has committed the crime though it offers the police no definite leads as to the identity of the murder at this early stage.

The profiler will also try to determine the killer's primary objective. Was murder the primary intention? Or was it a bungled robbery, which unexpectedly escalated to murder when the force the offender used to subdue the victim got out of hand? Alternatively, the killer may have struck as part of a sex attack, or for other emotional, selfish, or cause-specific actions which may relate to real or imagined slights. Or maybe the offender lashed out to counteract ill-treatment or violence in his or her own background from abusive parents, relatives, or siblings. Unpopularity either at school during childhood or later in life, an unsuccessful marriage, or an inability to hold down a job are all reasons for violence in the mind of the killer.

Some emotional intent crimes, where the perpetrator becomes convinced they have some kind of special relationship with their target, can involve an element of assassination rather than random murder, like the killings of celebrities such as President John F. Kennedy and singer John Lennon. Similarly, some sex crimes, like those of Jack the Ripper in Victorian London, may involve more than just the criminal's need to possess his victim sexually, but a drive toward mutilation or dismemberment.

Did killer and victim know one another?

Another important factor which may emerge from studying the crime scene is the likelihood of whether or not the victim and the murderer knew one another. From the information known about the victim — including age, lifestyle, work, physical fitness, and strength, and in some cases race and religion — profilers can determine whether he or she was a high-risk victim, a medium-risk victim, or a low-risk victim.

High-risk victims are those who are probably deliberately targeted by their attacker, who will seek them out and identify them in locations and at times when he or she knows that potential victims can be found. These victims often include prostitutes, the homeless, women living on their own, children, or the elderly, whose relative lack of physical strength makes them vulnerable. As for the locations, these can include busy but anonymous locations like bus depots and train stations, or isolated places where potential victims are more vulnerable.

Not all real-life cases fall neatly and completely into one extreme or the other. They represent the two extremes of a seamless continuum which will be covered in more detail later. However, most cases which do not fit either extreme completely will show a combination of some signs hinting at an organized killer with other signs pointing to a less organized individual, and the profiler's skill lies in using that balance to point to a more accurate profile of the person responsible.

At the opposite end of the scale, low-risk victims include those whose work and lifestyles do not suggest they were deliberately targeted as potential victims, and who were possibly unknown to the killer. In many cases this might not be obvious in a single case, purely because of that random element. In the case of a serial killer though, the combination of signs which point to a single individual being responsible for a series of killings, with a completely random and varying series of victims would carry this message very strongly. In cases like these, the only common factor linking the victims was that each of them was unlucky enough to have been in the wrong place at the wrong time.

In parallel with the level of risk represented by the victim, profilers also try to estimate the risk to which the killer was subjected in committing the crime. Here, an attack on a targeted individual whose daily routine may involve them walking through a quiet or secluded location chosen by the criminal as an ideal crime scene, would represent a low risk to the killer. On the other hand, snatching a victim from a busy street, with an abundance of potential witnesses, represents a very high risk, and here too details of the crime scene carry their own message to the profiler.

The geography of the area in the vicinity of the crime scene can also help to tell profilers more about the attacker's background. For instance, if the location is secluded and well away from public access, this can suggest local knowledge of the area, which may indicate the attacker lives in the district. In cases where the crime scene is close to road access but remote from public transport services, this strongly suggests the culprit has his own transport, especially if the body was taken away after the killing, to remain missing or to be found elsewhere.

One of the most important factors in assessing the risk to the criminal is the amount of time spent at the scene of the crime, which also helps to identify the type of person involved. How long would it have taken to subdue and kill the victim? How much time was spent at the scene with the victim's body? What was done to it? What forces drove the offender to do what he or she did? How much time was spent disposing of the body, either at the scene or elsewhere?

Time is important in another sense, too. Both the time and the day of the week the attack took place, together with the remoteness or otherwise of the location can suggest something about the daily routine of the criminal. Is the person employed, and, if so, how much freedom does he or she have during the working week?

Serial killings invariably attract the most publicity and demand the highest priority from the investigators involved in trying to solve them and catch the perpetrator. Sadly, each new victim that falls prey to the killer adds to the tragic toll of human life, but in many cases each additional crime also helps throw some light on the individual involved, and the workings of his or her mind. For example, in cases where crimes seem to be committed as part of a series by the same individual, do they begin showing escalation from sexual attacks to progressively more violent rapes, finally culminating in murder? Or where a serial killer is already at work, do the killings show signs of escalation, where the violence used against the victim in the killing itself, or the degree of mutilation carried out on the victim after death increases in intensity? The way the crimes develop can assist the profiler to determine what

OPPOSITE
Searching the victim's body for details to trap the killer – a medical examiner carries out an autopsy.

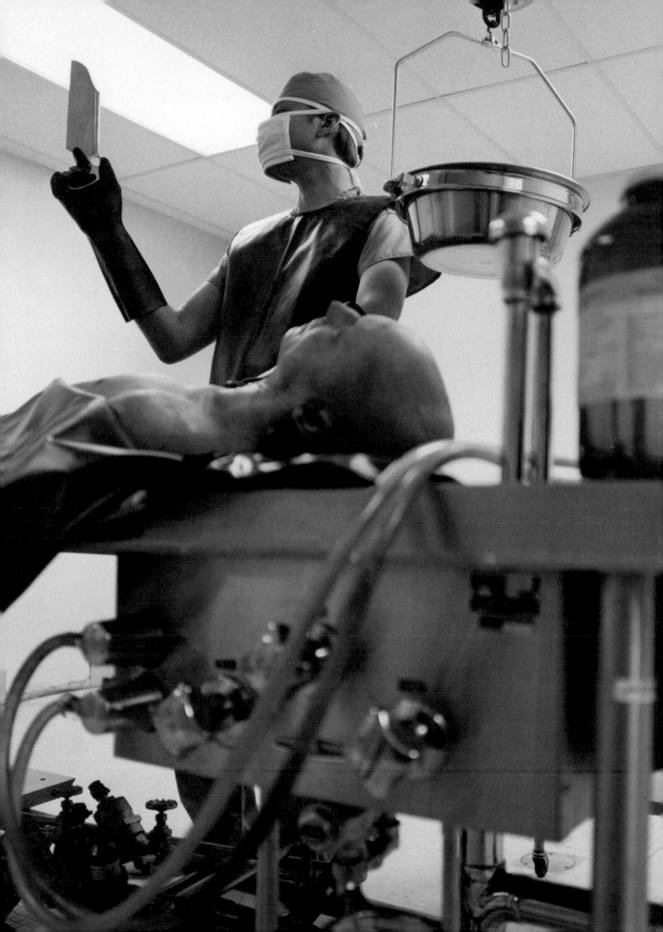

state of mind the killer is in and even predict if, when, or where he or she will next strike.

Weapons — and trophies

For many offenders, an important part of the crime is the taking of trophies which they use to relive the details of the assault in their own mind after the attack. Sometimes these can include the victim's personal possessions, items of clothing or underwear, or even body parts. Items which are clearly missing from the crime scene such as items of the victim's clothing or the weapon used to inflict wounds on the victim can still help throw light on the killer's motivation and on his personality type. If the victim's body remains at the scene, is it left in plain view or wholly, or partly covered? What position was it left in? Alternatively, if the body was removed from the scene, then the site where it was eventually ditched may offer more information, and may even be a spot where the killer returns to relive the details of the crime.

Post-mortem information is important to the profiler, but in a different way from its value to the police investigators. The post-mortem will reveal how the victim was killed — say either by a blunt, heavy instrument, or by strangulation. The identity of the blunt instrument and its present whereabouts, or the origin of the material used to strangle the victim is vital forensic evidence, since it can help tie the crime to an individual suspect, and can assist the profiler in understanding the psychological makeup of the criminal.

For the profiler, however, the type of weapon used is only the beginning. Identification of the type of weapon then produces a series of additional questions, all of which help narrow down the search for the criminal responsible. Whichever weapon was used, did the murderer bring it with him or was it an improvised object found at the scene, and possibly even left there afterward? In the former case, this is a sign of an organized killer. In the latter case, the signals point to a disorganized killer. Did the forensic evidence reveal the killer murdered the victim face-to-face, or was it a surprise attack carried out from cover? Face-to-face killing implies the murderer wanted to personalize the victim, and that, in the case of an organized killer, the victim was known to the attacker, rather than the more anonymous crime of someone who strikes without the victim being aware of what is happening until rendered incapable of fighting back. But all these signs have to be treated with care, since the criminal might have been deliberately trying to put the investigators off the scent, by trying to stage a different type of crime from the one actually committed.

Tell-tale signs of a staged crime

Finally, profilers learn to examine a crime scene to determine whether or not the killer tried to set a scene deliberately, to put the investigators on the wrong track by trying to portray the murder as a different kind of crime. This is called "staging" and its effectiveness depends on how knowledgeable the killer is about what would be found at the crime scene in a case of the type he is trying to suggest as a cover for his own deeds.

Murderers who kill a close relative or a member of their own family often try to suggest that some unknown attacker was responsible. They may try to stage the evidence of a robbery to add weight to their story, but usually inconsistencies will reveal to a profiler what really happened (*see* Case Study 5, page 61). In some cases, where robbers appear to have ransacked a house, taking away valuable possessions, investigators will find, more often than not, that items of real sentimental value which would be impossible to replace, miraculously seem to evade the criminals' attention.

For example, an emergency call to the police in Wilkes-Barre, Pennsylvania, in the early hours of Sunday morning, August 30, 1986, summoned them to the home of the Wolsieffer family at 75 Birch Street. There they found 33-year-old local dentist Dr. Edward Glen Wolsieffer lying on the floor, apparently suffering from the effects of a blow to the head and an attempted strangulation. Tending him was his brother Neil, who lived across the road from him. He told the police officers that his brother Glen had called him saying he was suffering from the effects of a violent attack. It was Neil who then made the call to the police.

The brothers also told the officers that Glen's wife, Betty Jayne Wolsieffer and their daughter, five-year-old Danielle, were somewhere upstairs.

Neither had been seen by the brothers since the attack. Whenever Neil had attempted to look for them, Glen had urged his brother to stay with him, and complained of feeling faint and expressed fears that the intruder who had attacked him might still be on the premises. The officers immediately searched upstairs, where they found Danielle asleep and unharmed in her own room. Her mother, however, was lying dead on the floor of the master bedroom. She had clearly been strangled, and there were bloodstains on the bed sheets. However, her face had been wiped clean, but though her nightdress had been pulled up over her waist, she was found not to have been sexually assaulted.

Glen Wolsieffer's story was that he and his wife had been in bed, when at first light he thought he had heard the noise of an intruder in the house. Without waking his wife, he had taken a handgun from the bedside table and crept out of the bedroom to check. As he emerged onto the upstairs landing, he saw a tall and heavily built man standing at the top of the stairs. The intruder seemed unaware of Wolsieffer watching him, and he was able to follow the intruder downstairs, but then he lost him in the darkness of the ground floor of the house. He began searching the rooms one by one, but was suddenly seized from behind with a cord around his throat, forcing him to drop the gun and fight for his life. He managed to break the intruder's grip and kick him in the crotch but he was then struck with a massive blow to the head which knocked him out. When he woke up, he was feeling so disoriented that all he could do was call his brother and ask for help.

Facts that didn't fit the story

To the investigators, a whole list of factors didn't add up. Though Wolsieffer did have signs of having suffered a blow to the back of the head, and some marks to the back of the neck with scratches to the left side of his chest, these seemed to be relatively trivial, compared with the violence of the apparent assault. But the most telling signs of a staged crime were those concerning Betty Wolsieffer and the intruder himself. First of all, a ladder left leading to an open upstairs window suggested where the attacker had entered the house. But why go to the trouble to climb to an upstairs window in growing daylight, in the view of neighbors and

BELOW
John Douglas, FBI profiler, spotted inconsistencies in Glen Wolsieffer's account of a botched burglary which revealed the crime had been staged in an attempt to conceal the fact he had murdered his wife.

passers-by? Having gained entry to the upstairs floor of the house the intruder apparently descended the stairs to the ground floor, where he found Dr. Wolsieffer, armed and searching for him. He attacked Dr. Wolsieffer and rendered him unconscious and then apparently went back upstairs without stealing even the jewelry in plain view in the bedroom. With an armed man downstairs and liable to regain consciousness at any time he decided to stop to kill Mrs. Wolsieffer, though he managed to do it without waking the child sleeping nearby, after which he left the house without taking anything.

The physical evidence added to their confusion. The ladder was too flimsy to support anyone of average weight, the rungs were facing the wrong way, there were no indentations in the soft ground at the base of the ladder to show any weight had been placed on it, and there were no signs of the dew and grass which the intruder would almost certainly have left on rungs or window ledge. There were no signs of pressure being applied to the front of Dr. Wolsieffer's neck, and his story was changing under questioning, from one intruder to two, while there was increasing evidence that his wife had decided to confront him about a series of affairs with other women.

The police decided to call in FBI profiler John Douglas to analyze the crime scene and profile the likely attacker to check out Wolsieffer's story. Douglas quickly concluded that this was indeed a staged crime, since none of the story of a burglary gone wrong would actually stand up. First of all, breaking into a house in a busy neighborhood in early daylight, at a weekend when there were two cars parked in the drive, would be a very high risk for any burglar. Entering through an upstairs window in these circumstances made no sense at all, and having done so, a burglar would always check out the upstairs rooms before heading downstairs.

There was nothing to show the intruder had brought any weapons with him, which meant he had not planned to kill anyone, and the evidence showed that Mrs. Wolsieffer had not been sexually attacked. However, she had been strangled face-to-face, a highly personal crime which didn't fit with the idea of a burglar trying to silence a potential threat, without taking anything of value. Most significant of all, the criminal had apparently left a powerfully built and armed man downstairs while attacking and killing an unarmed woman who represented a much less serious threat to him. Finding the evidence to pin down the dentist took time. At last, more than three years after the murder and following a move to Virginia, Glen Wolsieffer was finally arrested in November 1989 for the killing of his wife, and later found guilty of third degree murder.

Kidnapping — or murder?

In another type of staged crime, one of the few killings which involve women more frequently than men, a parent may try to stage a kidnapping to cover up the murder of a child. Here, too there are danger signs which can alert profilers that an apparent kidnapping is actually a cover up for an altogether simpler case of murder or assault. On the evening of October 25, 1994, 23-year-old Susan Smith who was going through a divorce from her husband, stopped at an intersection controlled by traffic lights at Monarch Mills, near the town of Union in South Carolina. There, she claimed to have been attacked by an armed black man, who appeared out of the darkness without warning, and jumped into the passenger seat. He threatened her and forced her to drive some four miles to the north-east of Union, past a signpost for a local landmark, the John D. Long Lake, where he ordered her out of the car and drove off with her two young sons, Michael and Alexander, still in the vehicle. Susan ran to a nearby house where she was able to call her family and the local police.

Once again, police began noticing inconsistencies. The lights-controlled intersection at Monarch Mills was normally at green, and only changed to red when triggered by a vehicle emerging from the side road. There had been no other traffic at the scene, according to Susan's own statement, which begged the question

ABOVE
Susan Smith, with her husband David at a press conference held to speed the search for the missing children – investigators noticed her apparent grief seemed unconvincing.

TOP RIGHT
Police mugshots of Susan Smith following her arrest and conviction for the murder of her sons.

OPPOSITE
Police divers retrieve Susan Smith's car, found upside down at the bottom of a local lake with the bodies of her sons inside.

as to why Susan had stopped there and made the hi-jacking possible. Furthermore, the investigators noticed she showed few of the signs of grief and agitation of a mother whose young children were missing. She made crying noises but showed no tears, and at one point referred to her boys in the past tense, as if she knew they were already dead. Facts also emerged about her very complex emotional life, including a relationship with a wealthy man in the area who represented an escape from the poverty which had dogged her life, and what she felt to be a restricted and humdrum existence. Finally, Roy Paschal, the forensic artist who had drawn a sketch of the hijacker with Susan's help, said she produced only a vague description but was very picky about some of the small details in his drawing, which suggested to him she was trying to cover up an invention rather than a recollection.

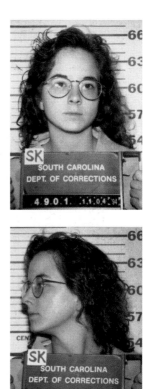

Here, too, the local police called in the FBI to provide them with a profile of the type of criminal who could possibly have harmed or even killed the young boys. The resulting blueprint fitted Susan Smith with uncanny accuracy. Based on their experience the FBI said the most likely perpetrator would be a young woman who had grown up in a background where poverty was a problem, had a poor education, and a history of physical or sexual abuse in childhood, was cut off from a social support

ABOVE
Susan Smith, following her arrest for the murder of her sons – she later confessed to killing them and was sentenced to 30 years to life for their murders.

network and was prone to depressive and suicidal tendencies, with a strong likelihood of being rejected by a male lover as the trigger of a desperate act against her own children. Susan's own father, to whom she had been specially close, had committed suicide after his marriage to Susan's mother had ended in divorce, and her father-in-law had attempted suicide as a consequence of another family marriage break-up, when Susan had found him and had to call the emergency services.

Suspicion had fallen on the lake near which the car had apparently been hijacked, but police frogmen had searched the bottom with no success. When the profile added to increasing

LEFT
The slope down to the lake where Susan Smith had allowed her car to roll into the deep water with her sons strapped inside and unable to escape.

concerns about Susan Smith's demeanor, police returned to search the whole area within walking distance of the house from which she had called the police, again without success. Susan herself was questioned more closely, with greater emphasis on the inconsistencies of her story, and eventually, nine days after the children's disappearance, she admitted having driven down to the edge of the lake, intending to drown herself and her children.

Finally, she had climbed out of the car and released the handbrake, before closing the door and allowing it to roll down into the water. Paradoxically, because the car was moving slowly, with doors and windows closed, it took a relatively long time to fill with water and drifted well out into the lake before sinking. When police divers searched the lake bottom further from the bank than before, they found the dark red 1990 Mazda Protégé saloon lying upside down with the bodies of the two boys still strapped in their seats. Post-mortems confirmed they had drowned as the car had sunk below the surface and slowly filled with water, a prolonged and terrifying death. On July 27, 1995 Susan Smith was sentenced to thirty years to life for the two murders.

In another similar case FBI agent Gregg McCrary was called in to profile the person responsible for abducting the two-year-old daughter of a single mother. She had been taking the little girl shopping, but when leaving their apartment block to go to her car she claimed she was seized by stomach cramps. She was forced to use the bathroom in her own apartment, stopping only to tell her daughter to stay close and play quietly until she rejoined her.

When she emerged, three-quarters of an hour later, the little girl was nowhere to be seen. The only clue was one of her woolen mittens lying in the parking lot, and this caused her to panic. She called the police emergency number and told them her child had been kidnapped. The police moved quickly, well aware that time is vital in child abduction cases. Appeals were made through local newspapers, and at last a communication came from the kidnappers. A package arrived at the woman's home containing the matching mitten to the one left at the scene of the abduction. There was no ransom note, no return address, no sign as to who the kidnappers were, or what they wanted.

For Gregg McCrary, it was all too clear that the kidnapping had never happened, and that the woman had all too probably killed her own child. First of all, parents whose children have disappeared are invariably very reluctant to admit they have been abducted or kidnapped, preferring instead to accept any other explanation for their absence — to use the term in the first call to the police suggested the mother had already decided the scenario in her own mind. The length of time she had spent in the bathroom with her child at risk of real abduction did also not ring true. But the most powerful indicator that this was a staged crime was the package from the "kidnappers."

People who abduct children do so for three main reasons. They kidnap them for money, they take them for sexual reasons, or they snatch them to make up for the lack of a child of their own. Real-life kidnappers would want to make their demands and collect the ransom as quickly as possible, since the longer they hold the child, the greater the risk of discovery. They would never open proceedings to show they have the child without at least starting off the process of demanding and collecting the ransom. The other two types of abductor would almost never want to make any contact with the family at all.

Eventually McCrary was proved right, when the mother confessed to killing the child, and took the police to the body. Here too was clear evidence to a profiler that the likely killer was a parent, even without the confession. The child's body was found buried in woodland, wrapped up in a snowsuit and an outer blanket, covered by a plastic bag to protect her from the weather or from predators. To an experienced profiler, the care taken over the child's remains spoke eloquently not of anger and hatred, but of a mixture of love and guilt.

In the majority of these cases, the criminals simply lack the specialized knowledge that would be needed to convince professional investigators that the impression the criminals are trying to create is actually true. Because of this, they end up by revealing more about the identity of the person responsible — themselves — than they might have done had they not chosen to rely so heavily on staging a completely different type of crime which they hoped would lead the hunt in a different direction, away from them and in pursuit of a non-existent suspect.

Sam Sheppard

Classic "Staged" Murder

SOMETIMES A CRIME PROFILER may be involved in a case where the original perpetrator of the crime has already been caught and even punished. Usually these cases involve a measure of doubt which the insight of a profiler may be able to resolve. One of the best known is the Sam Sheppard murder case, which involved an osteopathic surgeon who lived in the Bay Village suburb of Cleveland, Ohio, with his wife Marilyn. In the early morning of July 4, 1954, police were called to the Sheppard house where they found a distraught Sheppard being tended by his next-door neighbor John Spencer Houk — upstairs in the bedroom was the body of Marilyn Sheppard who had been beaten to death.

Sheppard's story was that he had spent the night sleeping on a couch in the downstairs living room after falling asleep watching the late-night movie on TV, when he had been woken by his wife's screams. He was vague about the time this occurred, but said he had rushed up the stairs into the bedroom where his wife was sleeping. There he claimed to have been attacked and knocked unconscious by a white figure.

When he came to, he tried to take his wife's pulse, but could find no signs of life, and he then went to check his son was safely sleeping in another room. He then heard sounds downstairs which showed the intruder was still in the house. He rushed downstairs and chased a man whom he described as large and powerfully built, with "a good sized head and bushy hair" out of the house and on to the lakeside beach where in a second struggle, he was again rendered unconscious.

He regained consciousness for the second time outside on the beach at the side of Lake Erie. When he returned to the house he found his wife's body, after which he called the Houks, who then phoned the police. By this

ABOVE
The home of Sam and Marilyn Sheppard in Bay Village, a suburb of Cleveland Ohio on the edge of Lake Erie. This quiet neighborhood became the scene of a hideous murder and the center of a storm of controversy.

time it was just a few minutes before six o'clock in the morning.

Sheppard was seen as the prime suspect, especially when he was unable to give more than the vaguest of descriptions of his attacker. Though there was said to be no clear motive for him to kill his wife, he was tried and convicted of her murder and sentenced to life imprisonment. However, Sheppard's lawyer called in Dr. Paul Leland Kirk, Professor of Criminalistics at the University of California, Berkeley, to examine the evidence and he found some puzzling inconsistencies.

The prosecution had made much of spots of blood on Sheppard's watch, but the doctor had insisted that when he had found his wife his first act had been to take her pulse to determine if there were any signs of life. Dr. Kirk also found that part of the blood-soaked bed where the body lay was actually free of blood. He concluded that this was where the killer had stood to deliver the blows, and he would consequently have been completely soaked with his victim's blood. Though Dr. Sheppard's clothes showed a single diluted bloodstain on the knee of his trousers, there was nothing on the scale which would be expected to identify him as the killer.

In the meantime, Sheppard's lawyers pressed for a new trial on the grounds of prejudicial publicity. Finally, their request was granted and Sam Sheppard was retried in 1966, and acquitted of the murder. He was released but the murderer was never found.

Later, after Sheppard's death in 1970, the lawyers representing his estate then began a civil action against the state of Ohio for their client's wrongful arrest and imprisonment. This was the second time the defence in a case involving Sam Sheppard called in an outside expert. In this case it was FBI trained crime profiler Gregg McCrary, and his analysis drew a completely different picture from that created by Sheppard's lawyers.

McCrary was convinced that Sheppard had indeed murdered his wife, and had then deliberately staged the scene to suggest an outside attacker. Letters found after the murder had revealed that Marilyn had been about to sue him for divorce, on account of his having had a succession of affairs. This provided a possible motive for her death. However, Sheppard's lawyers produced a potential suspect, though not one named by Sheppard — five years after the murder a local odd-job man named Richard Eberling had been arrested for stealing from households where he had worked, and among the property recovered had been Marilyn's wedding ring. However, in McCrary's unshakable opinion, Sheppard had made the classic mistake common to killers who know too little about the appearance of a genuine crime scene — he had tried to suggest three different types of crime, a sexual attack, a drug-related crime, and a burglary which had escalated to violence.

His wife's body had been placed on the bed partially undressed with legs apart, in a

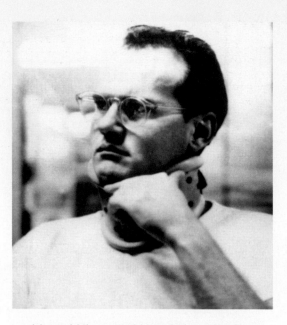

position which seemed intended to suggest a violent sex attack. However, there were none of the characteristic signs of internal damage which would have been caused by an attacker violent enough to assault her and then beat her to death. Many of the drawers of the bedside desk and dresser were pulled out to suggest a robbery, but the contents were carefully placed on the floor, whereas a real robber would have caused much more damage and chaos. Furthermore, nothing of any real value was missing. Although Sam's watch had been taken by the intruder, it was later found outside the house.

Finally, the suggestion of a drug-related robbery was made by Dr. Sheppard's medicine bag being left standing on end with some of its contents scattered around and, according to the doctor, some ampules of morphine missing. In genuine drug-related crimes the thief would invariably take the entire bag and escape as quickly as possible.

Even the attack delivered by the thief on Dr. Sheppard contained inconsistencies. To an intruder who had beaten his wife to death, he represented a direct threat to his successful getaway. However, instead of using similar violence on the husband of his victim, the killer simply dropped the murder weapon and hit the doctor with his fist. Sam Sheppard's injuries consisted of a bruise under one eye and a chipped tooth, whereas his wife had sustained

Dr. Sam Sheppard wearing a neck collar as a result of an injury he claimed he sustained from being attacked by the mysterious stranger he claimed had killed his wife.

LEFT
Sam Sheppard leaving court with his second wife Ariane following his acquittal for the killing of Marilyn at a retrial in November 1966.

RIGHT
FBI profiler Gregg McCrary provided crucial evidence that the crime scene had been staged, which helped defeat a civil action by Sheppard against the state of Ohio.

35 injuries, of which 20 were potentially fatal. To a crime analyst, the contrast between the murder of a less threatening individual while the individual who presents the biggest threat of capture or arrest to the intruder receives relatively minimal injuries is an almost infallible indicator of a staged murder scene.

On the question of the blood at the scene, McCrary concluded that Sheppard's claim that he could not have been the killer because he had so little blood on his person was inconsistent in the opposite direction. Given the amount of blood in the room, he would have been more bloodstained than he was, simply by checking his wife's pulse, as her arms, hands, and upper body were soaked in fresh blood and there must have been some blood traces on his hands and clothes. Furthermore, the spattering of blood on the watch was, in McCrary's opinion more consistent with sprays of blood droplets being thrown up when the blows were being delivered. This too suggested Sheppard was the killer, provided that he had hidden the watch as part of the staging, and used the time before he called the Houks to clean himself up thoroughly and dispose of any bloodstained clothing.

Furthermore, Sheppard had claimed he had fought with the killer who would then have been soaked with blood. There were also no signs of blood in the rest of the house, including objects which the killer would have touched, like the ransacked medical bag, the drawers which were opened, and the doors through which he made his escape.

One more sign of a staged killing was, in his view, significant. Many criminals who commit a murder and then try to present themselves as an innocent witness who discovered the crime do so by calling someone other than the police in the first instance. In this case, Sheppard called his friend, the local mayor, rather than the police.

Gregg McCrary's conclusions were that this was definitely not a sexually sadistic type of killing, which would have involved the murderer keeping his victim alive for as long as possible, to enjoy her suffering. Richard Eberling was an unlikely suspect in this type of killing as he was a lifelong homosexual. He remained convinced that the murder had been committed by Sheppard himself, who had then done his utmost to alter the details of the crime scene to throw suspicion on an unknown attacker. After ten weeks, the trial was completed and the jury reached a unanimous verdict. The state of Ohio won its case, though Sheppard himself was dead, and the action a civil one rather than a criminal action. The jury had concluded that Sheppard had not been falsely imprisoned, and no damages were owed to his family, though the controversy still rumbles on to this day, thanks to a whole series of conspiracy theorists.

Colin Pitchfork

DNA Traps the Murderer

IN NOVEMBER 1983 a 15-year-old schoolgirl named Lynda Mann was attacked, raped, and murdered in the Leicestershire village of Narborough, England. Her body was found in a secluded patch of woodland alongside a public footpath, not far from the Carlton Hayes Mental Hospital where psychologist Paul Britton had worked before being appointed senior clinical psychologist at Leicester General Hospital. Because of his specialized experience, Britton had already helped the police as a profiler in other rape and murder cases, and when in July 1986 another 15-year-old schoolgirl, Dawn Ashworth, was found raped and murdered in Narborough, they enlisted his aid once again. No-one had been caught for the murder of Lynda Mann, but Richard Buckland, a local 17-year-old youth working as a kitchen porter at Carlton Hayes, confessed to both killings.

On the face of it, there was definite evidence linking the suspect to the murder of Dawn Ashworth. His motorcycle was seen near the scene of the attack, alongside another footpath in the Narborough area, just five fields away from the spot where Lynda Mann's body had been found years before. Witnesses had also spoken of a man wearing a distinctive red crash-helmet, like that belonging to the suspect, and he had a history of less serious sexual offences.

One crucial discovery made it possible both to prove that Buckland's confession was false, and eventually to trap the real killer. At the time of the killings, Dr (now Sir) Alec Jeffreys had been working at Leicester University on a method for developing genetic markers from an individual's DNA as a form of biological barcode which could be compared with other specimens to show whether traces of body fluids did or did not come from that individual. When DNA extracted from the semen traces found on the bodies of the victims were compared, they showed positively that the same person had raped, and therefore presumably killed, both girls. On the other hand, when this DNA was compared with that extracted from a sample of Buckland's blood, the codes did not tally, proving that he was definitely not the

killer. He had simply given a false confession, a strange but surprisingly common occurrence in high profile murder investigations.

Paul Britton began by visiting both the murder scenes, and comparing the evidence of what had happened to the victims. Both girls had been attacked on a secluded footpath and had died from strangulation. In both cases their bodies had been moved through or over a gate to hide them from casual passersby. The first conclusion was that this was a local man, who knew his way around the neighborhood. Furthermore, he was not a 'loner' whose strange behavior might well have caused local people to develop suspicions, and to see him as a potential suspect. He had the confidence to approach the girls and remain in their company long enough to deliver his attack and render them helpless.

Britton suggested that the most likely attacker was someone older and more secure than Buckland, possibly in his late twenties, who had a reasonable level of education and who might well already be in a stable relationship. As he probably lived locally, he might well have been questioned by police during their door to door enquiries, when he must have been confident enough to reply without arousing their suspicions. His need for sexual control and domination which drove him to commit these murders would have been growing and developing over time, and the chances were strong that he would already have appeared in police records for less violent sexual offences, like indecent exposure. Most importantly, in spite of the details revealed in Buckland's confession, Britton was convinced that the killer had operated alone, and there was no question of the porter having been an accomplice.

Visits to the murder sites provided a possible explanation for Buckland's knowledge of the details of Dawn Ashworth's killing. It was clearly possible for someone in the area at the time to have witnessed the murder from the corner of a nearby field, close to a footbridge which crossed the M1 motorway (freeway). On the other hand, this left the police no closer to finding the real killer. To track down the murderer they decided to base the first ever mass DNA testing on the profile, by taking samples from all males aged between 14 and 34 at the time of the first murder living in Narborough and the adjacent villages of

Enderby and Littlethorpe. It was a massive operation, and yet it very nearly missed its target. More than 4,000 men provided blood samples, but none of them matched the DNA found on the victims' bodies. The records showed that one of the samples belonged to a 27-year-old worker at Hampshires Bakery in Leicester called Colin Pitchfork, with a wife and young son. He had indeed been questioned by the police earlier, but claimed to have been looking after his child while his wife had been at college at the time of the first murder, which helped to deflect suspicion.

Only in August 1987 did a fellow worker, Ian Kelly, reveal in a casual conversation in a Leicester pub that Pitchfork had bullied him into taking the blood test on his behalf, as Pitchfork had been worried because of an earlier conviction for indecent exposure. Another man present admitted that Pitchfork has approached him too, offering £200 if he would act as a stand-in, but he had refused. The remark was overheard by a manager at the bakery who passed on the information to the police. The police checked the signature on the sample against the one on the house to house enquiries and found they didn't match. Pitchfork was arrested, a sample of his blood was sent to Jeffreys' laboratory where the genetic barcode was found to be identical to that of the DNA sample from the killer.

Pitchfork's alibi proved accurate but insubstantial, as his son had been sleeping in a carrycot in the back of his car while he exposed himself to Lynda Mann and then attacked, raped, and finally killed her. In all the most important particulars the profile and the killer proved a perfect match. On January 22, 1988, Colin Pitchfork pleaded guilty to both murders and was jailed for life, and Ian Kelly received an 18-month suspended sentence.

CHAPTER FOUR

ORGANIZED OR DISORGANIZED?

4: Organized or disorganized?

CRIMINALS ARE AT LEAST AS COMPLEX as any other human beings, and much of the task of a profiler involves making a series of assessments based on the evidence presented by the type of crime, the location and scene of the crime, and the details of the victim. All these present the profiler with a series of questions which have to be answered before a useful profile can be generated. How old is the criminal likely to be? Is he well educated or poorly educated? Does he live locally, or outside the immediate area? Does he have personal transport, or not? But none of these questions is as important, or capable of revealing as much about the criminal, as the decision of whether the criminal is "organized," or "disorganized."

In the context of criminal profiling, the terms "organized" and "disorganized" have specialized meanings. They were developed by the FBI during the late 1970s as part of the evolution of criminal profiling into a reliable and effective technique which could be used by a wider spectrum of trained personnel rather than being confined to specialist and academically qualified psychologists. FBI profiler Roy Hazelwood referred in his book *The Evil That Men Do* to the ideas which helped him develop the concept in relation to a case involving two killers, James Clayton Lawson Jr. and James Russell Odom, a pair of violent sex attackers who had originally met in the mid-1970s when confined to a high-security state mental institution at Atascadero in California, and an interview between fellow profiler Bob Ressler with serial killer Jeffrey Dahmer (*see* Case Study 19, page 166).

Lawson and Odom spent much of their leisure time in the hospital discussing their fantasies of attacking young women. In Odom's case, the main objective was sex, but Lawson was less interested in raping his intended victims than he was in killing and mutilating them. The two were finally released on parole, whereupon Odom drove all the way to Columbia, South Carolina, where Lawson was working as a pipe fitter and living with his parents as a condition of his parole. Within days the pair went out looking for victims to allow them to act out their

ABOVE
FBI profiler Roy Hazelwood first developed the concept of "organized" and "disorganized" killers and the characteristic signs which enable analysts to tell them apart.

PREVIOUS PAGE
Recording evidence at the scene: a Russian crime photographer takes pictures of a murder victim in St. Petersburg.

Convicted murderer fails to get parole

S AUG 22 '85 THU

By SCOTT JOHNSON
State Staff Writer

Crime, murder:

James Clayton Lawson Jr., serving a life sentence for the 1975 murder and mutilation of a Richland County woman, was denied parole Wednesday.

Fifth Circuit Solicitor James C. Anders, other law enforcement officials and relatives of the victim told the state Board of Parole and Community Corrections Wednesday that Lawson should stay in prison.

Lawson was found guilty of premeditated murder in the slaying of Emily "Libby" Adkins Moyer. Mrs. Moyer, 25, was abducted about 1 a.m. on Aug. 28, 1975, from a Richland County convenience store on U.S. 1.

She was taken to a wooded area off Polo Road near Sesqui-Centennial State Park and raped. Her throat was then cut and her body mutilated.

Lawson was sentenced to death, but was resentenced to life in prison in 1977 after the state's capital punishment law was declared unconstitutional.

During the five-day trial, James Russell Odom, Lawson's accomplice, testified that the woman's death was the re-enactment of a fantasy he and Lawson had had at a California state mental hospital.

Odom pleaded guilty to rape, possessing an illegal weapon and being an accessory before and after the fact of murder. He was sentenced to life in prison plus 40 years.

Lawson offered the defense of insanity, but was found guilty of murder after 19 minutes of jury deliberation.

ABOVE
Serial killer Jeffrey Dahmer at his initial court hearing accused of four murders, though police are convinced this highly organized killer was responsible for the deaths of as many as seventeen victims.

LEFT
James Clayton Lawson Jr. was one of a pair of violent sex attackers who met his future partner in crime, James Russell Odom, while inmates at a high security mental institution in California. This newspaper coverage details his parole application in 1985, which was rejected.

fantasies in real life. Driving Lawson's father's car, they stopped at a Seven-Eleven store on a local highway, where they saw a 25-year-old woman working behind the counter, but were unable to attack her because there were too many people about.

They returned late the following night, bought a few items from the store including a knife, and then abducted the store assistant at gunpoint and took her to a secluded spot nearby. There they forced her to strip naked, and Odom raped her. He climbed out of the car for Lawson to take his turn, but the other simply killed her by cutting her throat and then cut off her breasts and mutilated her corpse. They left her in plain view, and took her clothes away with them. The police had already been called to the store which had been left open and unattended after they left with their victim, and the presence of money and the victim's belongings showed that robbery had not been the motive. The discovery of the corpse and witness statements mentioning the presence of Lawson's father's car at the scene soon led detectives to the killers, who admitted their guilt. Odom confessed to the rape but not the murder, and Lawson denied rape but admitted wanting to obliterate the girl as a person. Both Lawson and Odom were convicted.

Comparing these killers, it was clear to Hazelwood that the violent rape and murder of a young female assistant in a South Carolina convenience store was so unplanned and casually carried out that it seemed as if the killers were indifferent to being caught and punished for their crime. Compared with other killers who carried out equally stomach-churning crimes, these two attackers seemed to Hazelwood to be as disorganized as it was possible for them to be.

The careful killer
Jeffrey Dahmer on the other hand, was a very different prospect altogether. Though equally deadly and dangerous, he planned his killings with the greatest possible care. Not only did he work out every detail of an intended attack, but he even went to the trouble of rehearsing many of the moves involved. He would pick up a potential victim, try out an assumed personality and routine on him, and later release him without him even being aware of the danger he had faced. His intention had been to develop a conversational style and script which would be as effective as possible in persuading potential victims to trust him, to the point where he had them completely under his control, whereupon he was free to strike. Once he had persuaded them to accompany him back to his apartment, he clearly had the confidence to kill them there, and to keep body parts as trophies on open display, an act of appalling potential danger to himself should he ever fall under suspicion. However, in contrast to Odom and Lawson, Dahmer was a completely organized killer and in common with many organized killers, possessed supreme self-confidence, even to the point where it became extremely dangerous.

When the FBI profilers turned to applying the organized-disorganized distinction to the cases in their records, it was clear that this was an extremely valuable criterion for assessing the behavior of the perpetrator of a crime. In psychological terms, there was a clear distinction between the two. The disorganized criminal shows signs of a type of behavior which is clearly deranged and asocial, or psychotic, where his sense of reality becomes highly distorted. The organized criminal, on the other hand, behaves in a way which is outwardly sane, yet highly

OPPOSITE
Police mugshot of Jeffrey Dahmer, the classic organized killer who appeared outwardly sane and reasonable, in spite of his terrible secrets.

irrational, and ultimately antisocial, or psychopathic, and his lack of moral responsibility drives him to perform violent acts. For the profiler, these distinctions are extremely important, since they can clearly be deduced from the way in which a particular attack is planned and carried out. Once the killer can be assessed as an organized or disorganized personality — or sometimes a mixture of the two — then a series of very valuable deductions can be made about his background, his work, his location, his motivation, and his educational and employment record, all of which can help narrow down the search for the offender.

Signs of a disorganized killer

What kind of signs suggest to a profiler that a crime has been committed by a disorganized offender? The overall impression will be of a crime which has been committed suddenly, as the seizure of a target of opportunity, rather than a crime which has been planned and thought out carefully, with the object of ensuring that the criminal can escape detection. Often the crime scene itself will be chaotic and in total disarray, reflecting the haste of the killer to bring his victim under his control and render him or her incapable of further resistance. The killer's first anxiety is that his victim may evade his clutches, and therefore he frequently attacks without warning, from behind, to maximize his chances of surprise, or he kills instantly, usually with a knife or a gun. In most cases, the location shows that the victim is only at the scene because he or she lives or works there, as part of the victim's own routine, since the disorganized criminal lacks the confidence or the plausibility to persuade a potential victim to accompany him to a pre-planned location for the crime. Consequently, victims are usually not tied up or restrained, as they have been killed quickly.

Victims of disorganized killers are often battered especially violently about the face. This sometimes reflects a need for the killer to depersonalize his victim, or the fact that the victim might resemble someone in the killer's life for whom he feels fear or anger. Sometimes the victim will be blindfolded, or the face will be covered up, as part of the depersonalizing process. Where the killer carries out sexually sadistic acts like rape, mutilation, or even disembowelment, these will often have been done after the victim was already dead. If the body has been left at the crime scene, it will usually be in plain view, but some disorganized killers take the victim's remains with them, as trophies of the attack. Usually there will be an abundance of footprints and fingerprints, and in many cases the weapon will be one picked up at the scene, and discarded there afterwards.

Given that a crime reveals the hand of a disorganized killer, what can profilers deduce as a result of this diagnosis? The FBI research shows that disorganized killers are often below average in intelligence and are socially inadequate. Within a family they are usually among the younger children, with a father who combines harsh discipline with an unstable employment history. The criminals themselves are socially inadequate and sexually inexperienced, and also have a poor employment record in an unskilled job, after possibly dropping out of school. They tend to live on their own, or with an older family member, with minimal contact with people outside their immediate family, and often tend to go out only after dark.

They will often have poor personal hygiene, and low self-esteem. They show little or no interest in the news media in general, and they will tend to live or work near the scene of the crime. They either have no personal transport, or the vehicle they have will be old and badly maintained. Because they commit the crime under high levels of stress and anxiety, this can trigger a significant change in the criminal's behavior, which might involve increased use of drugs or alcohol, for example, or a turn to religion. They often return to the scene of the crime soon afterwards, to help them relive the details of the killing, and sometimes turn up at the victim's funeral or memorial services, even occasionally placing an "In Memoriam" message in the local newspaper, to perpetuate their control over the victim and their links to the victim's family. Some disorganized killers keep a detailed personal diary to describe their actions and their victims and to provide something to help relive the crimes afterwards.

Confidence and control — the organized killer
At the opposite end of the scale, what kind of crime scene suggests the work of an organized criminal to the profiler? In this case, there will be signs of the planning and care which the criminal has taken to avoid the threat of detection and identification. The location will be one which is likely to have been carefully chosen by the killer for its relative isolation and immunity from observation, and the victim may have been taken there, or in some cases may simply have arrived at the scene where the killer seized his opportunity and struck.

However, organized serial killers usually personalise their victims, in terms of selecting them according to a preference for a particular type of victim. Factors which will be important to the killer will include age, gender, appearance, occupation, and lifestyle, but may well involve details which would seem trivial to anyone else. Some organized serial killers have, bizarrely, confined their attacks to women being driven by a male friend, or even women driving two-door cars.

Part of the organized criminal's approach to the crime is to present himself as non-threatening to the victim, until he has the victim firmly under his control. He will usually be sufficiently socially confident to strike up a conversation, and will not appear as odd or suspicious as the disorganized criminal. He is usually above average height and weight, with an impressive appearance and clothing which is chosen to reassure — either a business suit, a uniform, or casual clothing which is neat and clean. Once he has succeeded in bringing the victim under his control he may well use his own, or his victim's car to transport them to the chosen crime scene.

In many cases, the organized killer will rape his victim before, or even instead of, killing her. Where murder occurs, the weapon will usually have been brought to the scene by the killer, and be taken away afterwards. There will be signs that the victim has been restrained with chains, ropes, belts, clothing, gags, or blindfolds, which will also have been brought by the killer, and usually removed afterwards. The body too will often be taken away, to be disposed of more carefully than the disorganized killer, with the objective of making discovery less likely.

BELOW
The smallest details can help trap a killer – a hair from murder victim Jessica Chapman, who was killed with her friend and schoolmate Holly Wells in Soham in Cambridgeshire, England, in the summer of 2003 by school caretaker Ian Huntley.

Organized, disorganized and mixed crime scene and offender characteristics

The information presented here is used as a preliminary basis when initiating a rape or murder investigation. In practice, all crime scenes are mixed to some degree but establishing which category a crime scene or offender falls under provides a starting point in the early stages of an investigation.

The crime scene

Crime characteristics	Offender type: Organized	Offender type: Disorganized
Victim selected	targeted	chosen at random
Attack	planned	unplanned
State of victim's body	hidden	disfigured
Sexual act committed	before death successful	after death unsuccessful
Weapons/props	brings with	finds at scene
Physical assault	torture	quick
Sophistication of the crime	high, refined with each attack	low
Trophy/souvenir taken	yes	sometimes
Follows crime in news	yes	no

A mixed crime scene may give evidence of an organized offender having been disturbed or of unexpected resistance from a victim, for example.

Similarities — and differences

One of the few similarities between organized and disorganized killers is that the organized killer, too, may return to the scene of the crime, to relive the sensations and excitement of the crime. However, unlike the disorganized killer, he is better able to change this aspect of his behavior if he decides this may heighten the risk to him personally. Nevertheless, the criminal's high level of confidence will often enable him to play a part on the fringe of the investigation by volunteering information to the police as a potential witness, with the intention of putting them off his trail, and by spending time in locations where off-duty police investigators tend to meet for a drink or a meal.

Another similarity between organized and disorganized killers is that they tend to have few genuine friends. Here the reasons are very different. The disorganized killer type will be alone because he is socially inept and feels inferior, but the organized killer will be a loner by choice, because he feels superior to others. Relative to the disorganized killer, he will be of average to above average intelligence, with a stable employment history in skilled or specialist work. He will also be sexually competent, and will usually be living with a partner on a long-term basis. In terms of family background, he will be among the older children, with a father in stable and usually well-paid work, with an inconsistent style of discipline. A common factor in the background of organized killers is early experience with drugs and alcohol.

Offender profile

Crime characteristics	Offender type: Organized	Offender type: Disorganized
Residence	further from crime	close to crime
Living arrangements	usually with partner	alone or with family
IQ	average or above average	low
Employment	skilled or specialist	menial or unemployed
Social competence	confident	loner
Childhood discipline	lax or inconsistent	harsh
Family background	among the older children in the family	among younger children
Father's work	stable	unstable

Organized killers usually have their own transport, which will normally be in good condition and well maintained. This enables them to plan to find their ideal crime scene location over a much larger area. They will also tend to keep in touch with the local newspaper and broadcast coverage of the crime, to enable them to monitor police efforts and keep in close touch with the level of threat to themselves. During the commission of the crime, the organized killer remains controled and afterward may well decide to change jobs or move to a different town as a precaution against being caught. Unlike the disorganized killer, his better education and greater confidence means he can easily transplant himself.

This was the first approach adopted by the FBI for classifying criminals on the basis of the signs shown by the way they approached and committed their crimes, and to use that classification to suggest their family, education, and employment history, their appearance and social standing, and a great deal of other information. As such it was, and still remains, extremely useful. More recently, though, it has been joined by other ways of throwing light on an individual crime from differing perspectives, to show up other factors of the criminal's character profile and help add detail to the picture which acts as a focus for the police search for the person responsible. These will be described in greater detail in later chapters of the book.

Robert Napper

The Green Chain Rapist

NOT ALL DISORGANIZED CRIMINALS are caught quickly. Sometimes a mixture of cunning and good luck can enable them to avoid being identified for long enough to notch up a string of victims before they are finally trapped. A series of sexual attacks and rapes of young women in South East London began on the morning of August 10, 1989, when a 30-year-old single mother was raped in her home in Plumstead by a masked intruder armed with a Stanley knife, a type of knife used for home DIY. He had entered through the back door of the house which had been left unlocked, had walked past her young children who had been playing downstairs while she was drying her hair in an upstairs room, and he had left after the rape. Apart from the rape itself, no violence had been used against the victim, and nothing had been taken from the house. Semen traces were taken for DNA profiling.

The attacker struck again on the evening of March 10, 1992, after a gap of two and a half years. A 17-year-old girl was walking home from visiting friends in Lewisham, some four miles from the first attack, when she was attacked from behind and threatened with a knife. The attacker attempted to rape her but failed to achieve penetration. He punched her in the face before the attempted rape and kicked her in the head several times afterward before leaving the scene. Traces of semen on her clothing yielded a DNA profile which matched that found at the first attack in Plumstead.

Eight days later in Eltham, two miles to the east of Lewisham, another 17-year-old was walking along a footpath in the early evening when an attacker wearing a mask and carrying a knife had attempted to rape her. He had removed his mask, threatened her, and actually inflicted a knife-wound to her breast which had caused some bleeding. DNA from semen traces linked this case to the earlier two attacks. However, this time the victim was able to help police artists produce a likeness of the attacker.

The locations of the first and third attacks had one link in common. They were both close to a system of footpaths linking parks and open spaces in South East London called the Green Chain Walk, which would figure again in the fourth of the attacks, on the afternoon of

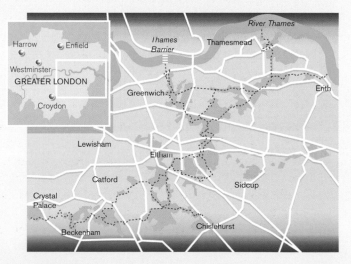

RIGHT
Map of the Green Chain Walk network of footpaths in south east London which linked the attacks by the Green Chain rapist.

Sunday May 24, 1992. A 22-year-old mother was pushing her two-year-old daughter in a buggy along a section of the path when she was attacked violently from behind, with a cord of some kind pulled round her neck and a series of heavy blows to her head and upper body. The attacker then partially undressed her before attempting to rape her, then leapt to his feet and ran off. Semen traces linked this attack to the earlier three, as the work of the criminal now becoming known as the Green Chain Rapist.

Three other sightings, including an attack which failed because of the violent response from one of the victim's dogs were also thought to involve the same criminal. At this point, the police called in profiler and forensic psychologist Paul Britton, who began by examining the first attack, which had differed in many respects from those which followed it. First of all, it had been indoors rather than outside in a very public space, and represented a different kind of opportunity for the rapist. He must have known his victim was there, on her own apart from her young children, and with the door unlocked. Furthermore, there was the gap of more than two years after this attack,

when criminals of this type normally attack women at much more frequent intervals, as had been the case with later assaults.

All four victims were young and attractive women, which suggested to Britton that the attacker was concentrating on victims of a particular type — not so much in purely physical appearance as in the degree of apparent vulnerability they showed. He decided the attacker was likely to be 28 or under, and most probably in the age range of between 20 and 25. This he based on the attacker's sexual inexperience and his relative familiarity with local footpaths and bus routes. He had clearly behaved impulsively, though he had managed to evade capture so far. Britton concluded he was below average intelligence, with a fairly menial job and a degree of sexual dysfunction.

His choice of location for the later attacks confirmed he was prone to take risks, though in time he could well refine his methods of selecting and approaching his victims to make it less likely he would be caught. He clearly did not mind inflicting pain on his victims, though this seemed to fall short of outright sadism, where the inflicting of pain became the primary objective of the attack.

The exception was in the earliest attack where he had operated coolly and methodically. This suggested to Britton that he might have had experience in entering other people's houses, possibly in carrying out burglaries. On the other hand, attacking his other victims in the open air is often linked with an earlier history of indecent exposure or peeping-Tom behavior, and he suggested the criminal might well already be known to the police for either type of offence. He also emphasized that there was a danger of the violence used in the attacks escalating to the point where a victim might be killed unless the attacker was caught fairly speedily.

The truth of this prediction was borne out in November 1993, when 27-year-old Samantha Bissett and her four-year-old daughter Jazmine were found in their Plumstead flat on November 4. Samantha was naked, and her chest had been sliced open and the rib cage pulled apart to display her internal organs, though the absence of large amounts of blood showed this had been done after her death. Jazmine had been undressed, sexually assaulted, put back in her clothes, and then smothered with her pillow.

The post-mortem confirmed that part of Samantha's lower abdomen was missing, probably taken by the killer as a trophy. She had been killed by stabbing, but most of the wounds inflicted after death concentrated on her breasts and genital regions. Once again Paul Britton was called in to advise the police, and he estimated the age of the killer as around 25 years, with a previous history of escalating sexual offences including rape or the threatening of violence against victims or prostitutes. The anger he showed in the violence of the damage done to his victim reflected his rage against women and his lack of success with them.

At last in May 1994, police were able to match bloodstained fingerprints found in the Bissetts' flat with strikingly similar prints belonging to 28-year-old Robert Clive Napper, who worked at a local plastics factory and lived in a flat in Plumstead High Street. He had been arrested a year before when he had tried to persuade a local printer to copy official Metropolitan Police stationery. Police who searched his flat found unlicensed firearms and

later street maps of the area with many of the rape and attack sites highlighted, while a DNA test revealed he was also the Green Chain rapist. As Paul Britton had predicted, he had a record of menial jobs, and had appeared in police files for low-level sexual offences like trying to peep into windows of houses where young women lived. Both of Britton's profiles had been accurate, but the time taken to catch the criminal allowed the person described in the first attack to mutate into the much more dangerous and violent subject of its successor. Finally in October 1995 Napper admitted to the manslaughter of the Bissetts and to two rapes and an attempted rape in 1992 and was sentenced to life imprisonment.

OPPOSITE
Part of the Green Chain Way system of signposted footpaths across a wide swathe of south east London.

ABOVE
Profiler Paul Britton predicted that the escalating level of violence in the attacks made it likely that the rapist would eventually kill his victims.

Robert Hansen

Ice-cold Killer

PERHAPS ONE OF THE MOST BIZARRELY organized killers of all was found to be operating in the remote wilderness of Alaska in the early 1980s. Police had originally been alerted on June 13, 1982 by a 17-year-old prostitute with a handcuff hanging from one wrist, who had run up to a patrol officer at Anchorage airport and told an extraordinary tale. She had been picked up by a short, red-haired man who had offered her $200 to give him oral sex in his car. While she was doing so, he had slipped the handcuff on her wrist and forced her at gunpoint to go with him to his house. There he had stripped her and raped her, biting her nipples and inflicting other injuries before handcuffing her to a pole and leaving her there while he went off for several hours' sleep. When he returned he told her he had been so pleased with her he was going to fly her to his log cabin in the woods for more sex, then bring her back to town and let her go.

By this time she was all too well aware of her mortal danger. She'd seen her attacker's face clearly, and could easily identify him, and she assumed she would not be simply brought back to town and left in safety. He forced her back into the car and they drove to the airport, where he began loading supplies into his light aircraft. She seized her only opportunity for escape and ran off to tell her story to the first policeman she found.

To the police her description suggested a married man in his middle forties named Robert Hansen. He had grown up in Iowa but had moved to Anchorage in 1965, where he ran

BELOW
The airport at Anchorage in Alaska where Hansen kept his Piper Cub light aircraft he used to transport his victims out into the wilderness where he hunted and killed them.

OPPOSITE
The Knik Glacier where the body of one of Hansen's victims was found, dead from wounds inflicted by a hunting rifle.

a successful bakery business. He had a son and a daughter and owned a Piper Super Cub aircraft which he kept at the local airport. The victim of the attack identified his house as the place where she had been raped and confined, and the aircraft as the one belonging to her attacker.

Hansen chose to deny everything, claiming that he was well known in the community as a successful businessman and the young prostitute was simply attempting to extort money from him. His wife and children were away at the time of the attack, but he had an alibi, as he said he had been dining with two business colleagues, both of whom confirmed his story.

Nevertheless, earlier discoveries began to ring several mental alarm bells among the local police. In 1980 they had found the bodies of two women in different places in the wilderness. One belonged to an unknown victim whose corpse had been half eaten by bears, and the other was named Joanne Messina, whose body was found in a gravel pit.

In September 1982 hunters at a remote stretch of the Knik River found the remains of 23-year-old topless dancer Sherry Morrow. She had been buried in a shallow grave, and had died from wounds inflicted by a high-powered Ruger hunting rifle, a common weapon in the area. More confusingly, there were no bullet holes in the clothes in which the body was dressed, which suggested she had been naked when she was shot.

In the late summer of 1983, the body of another topless dancer named Paula Golding was found in a shallow grave along the same river as Sherry Morrow. She too had been shot with a Ruger rifle, as revealed by the shell casings found near her body. The police were now convinced that these crimes had something to do with Robert Hansen, who was known locally as a skilled and experienced hunter, but before trying to obtain a warrant to search his home, they needed a better idea of the kind of signs they should be looking for.

They called in FBI profiler John Douglas for advice, in what he described as the first time a profiler had been used to support a search warrant. His first reaction was that all the victims and the potential victim who had escaped were all on the fringes of settled society. Working as prostitutes and topless dancers meant they would follow a transient and nomadic lifestyle which suggested they would not be missed easily or quickly if they disappeared. A local man like Hansen would know this, and it was likely he targeted each one deliberately.

Hansen himself was short and slight, with pockmarked skin and a pronounced stutter, all of which suggested to Douglas that he would have had severe problems with girls as a teenager, and in spite of his marriage might still harbor a great deal of resentment against women in general. His hunting experience also suggested, in this particular case, that he might be using the idea of hunting and killing animals as a way of exerting control which he had not previously been able to do with humans.

But did this mean he was hunting down his victims in some way? The fact that most of his victims were prostitutes or exotic dancers suggested he might find them easy to approach, and expendable enough to use them as human game. Douglas concluded that in the early murders, Hansen could have used the aircraft and the wilderness as a convenient way of disposing of the victims of pure anger attacks, and only later did the killer refine his fantasy to the point where he stripped his captives naked and released them into the wild, before hunting them down and killing them with his rifle in the ultimate act of revenge.

So what should the police look for in the Hansen household? Douglas was convinced the Ruger rifle was vitally important to Hansen, and it would be placed out of public view, in a safe hiding place within the house. He would almost certainly have trophies on the wall from the animals he had shot, but the nearest equivalent from his human victims would be items of jewelry, and possibly photos or other possessions or even items of underwear. The police also re-interviewed Hansen's business colleagues, warning them of the consequences to them if they had lied to give Hansen a false alibi. They admitted they had been asked to cover his story as a favor to a friend, which gave the police the leverage they needed to take out a search warrant and examine the suspect's house.

There they found the Ruger rifle hidden from view, and ballistics tests confirmed it had been used in the shootings of two of the victims. They also found a huge collection of animal

ABOVE
Anchorage bakery owner Robert Hansen finally admitted to killing 17 women over a ten year period and disposing of their remains in remote wilderness country.

trophies and, much more significantly, items of jewelry, a watch, and ID cards from the victims, hidden under the floor of one of the bedrooms, and a pilot's chart of the region with locations of the bodies marked on it.

When arrested, Hansen still denied he had committed any of the murders, claiming that the ballistic evidence could have resulted from his having been hunting in the area while unaware of the presence of the bodies. Only when the prosecution made it clear they would be pursuing the death penalty unless he admitted his guilt, did he finally confess. On February 27, 1984 Hansen finally entered a guilty plea for four murders, one rape, one kidnapping, and a list of theft and firearms charges. He was sentenced to a total of 499 years in prison.

CHAPTER FIVE:
COMMUTERS, MARAUDERS, AND VICTIMS

5: Commuters, marauders, and victims

The FBI's system of distinguishing between organized and disorganized killers provided a useful set of benchmarks for profilers to use in deciding the type of criminal who was responsible for a particular crime, from the evidence which showed how the criminal had actually behaved. More recently, though, other criteria have been developed to help shed more light on the criminal from a number of different perspectives. This trend was already becoming apparent in British profiler Paul Britton's work relating to the Green Chain Rapist (*see* Case study 7, page 77) and in David Canter's unraveling of the case of John Duffy, the Railway Rapist (*see* Case study 4, page 42). In many ways the plotting of the locations of Duffy's attacks and the correlation of his own address with the area in which he operated, along with the relevance of local public transport networks, set a pattern for future developments in what became known as geographical profiling.

Professor Canter's research focused on trying to work out what had happened before a criminal committed the first of a series of crimes rather than predicting where he might have gone after his most recent offence. The reasoning was that an individual criminal was more vulnerable to being caught early in his career than he was after time and experience had refined his method of operating to leave fewer loopholes. In theory the same principles which governed where a potential rapist or killer would travel to search for victims or carry out attacks, would operate in the cases of lesser crimes like burglary, and one of Canter's research students carried out a project which involved working with a local police force in examining the records of 32 convicted burglars, who had each committed between five and 70 burglaries before being caught.

By plotting the locations of each of an individual burglar's crimes on a large scale map it became clear that all the crimes tended to fit within a very restricted geographical area which included the burglar's own home. At this level, it was undeniable that crime for each individual felon was an essentially local business. Furthermore, it was also established that where a line was drawn on the map between the locations of the crimes which were furthest apart, and this line was used to define the diameter of a circle, most of that criminal's crimes would fall within that circle. In addition, the location of the burglar's home tended to be near the center of that circle. In other words, in the absence of any other geographical factors like river crossings or other barriers which would limit access in any particular direction, criminals tended to operate within a given range in almost all directions, working outwards from their base.

How criminals operate

Professor Canter set out to explain this phenomenon by understanding how criminals operated in relation to their fixed base. They would be more likely to carry out their crimes in an area they knew well, with its understood dangers and the possibility of escape routes. On the other hand, they would not want to operate too close to home because of the danger of being caught, or recognized, or even being involved in police house-to-house enquiries around the scene of the crime. This suggested they would begin by moving a certain minimum distance from their base to carry out their first crime, but not so far that they risked moving out of familiar territory.

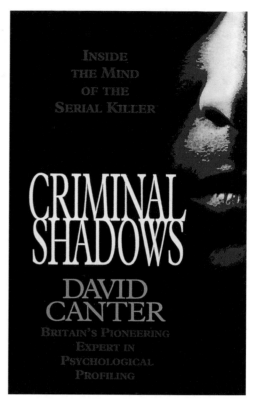

ABOVE
Cover shot of *Criminal Shadows*, Professor David Canter's study of the motivation and psychology of serial killers.

Assuming the first crime is successful, they then try to repeat the experience. It is unlikely they will re-offend near to the scene of the first crime, as it seems logical to expect the hue and cry to have made people in that area more vigilant, and perhaps police surveillance to have been stepped up. Nevertheless, the original thinking which governed the ideal distance from his base, while still remaining inside familiar territory, will still govern his thinking. Consequently, the second crime is likely to take place at a similar distance from his base, but in a different direction from the first crime. The same argument probably holds true for crimes number three and four, and the likelihood is that these will all be in markedly different directions from the base.

By the time the criminal commits crime number five, the geographical distribution of the earlier crimes is likely to channel his efforts back into the neighborhood of the original crime, since the other areas within his reach will have been raided more recently. The end result is that as more and more crimes are committed, they will all tend to lie within the boundaries of a circle, with the base at the center. Other geographical factors like natural barriers, open spaces, location of police stations, and the distribution of potential targets will all tend to distort the picture slightly, but the overall mechanism continues to hold good.

Finding the criminal's base

If this could be shown to be true in examining the records of known and convicted criminals, then could it help reveal the likely location of a criminal's base, where only the locations of the crimes were known, but not the identity of the person who committed them? Canter applies the principle to the crimes of Jack the Ripper (*see* Introduction, page 10) and on that basis

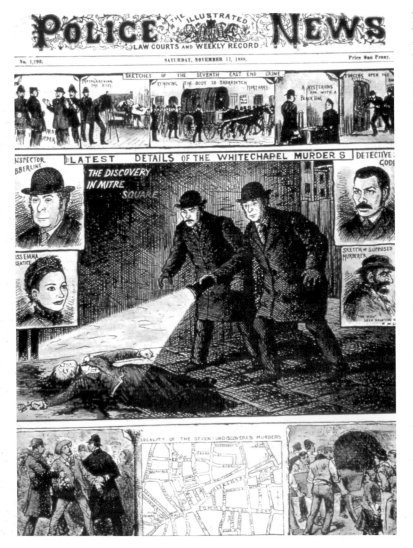

LEFT
The huge public interest, and the widespread climate of fear at Jack the Ripper's series of killings in the East End of Victorian London was fed by the lurid details quoted in periodicals like the *Illustrated Police News.*

tends to agree with the FBI profilers' assumption that Aaron Kosminski was at least a promising subject, since his base (in the form of the house of his brother Wolf, who had assumed responsibility for Aaron and looked after him before he was committed to a mental hospital) lay close to the circle which could be drawn around the sites of the five Ripper murders.

As with other aspects of profiling, different human beings may think along broadly similar lines but reach different conclusions when other factors are involved. Burglars who operate in densely populated areas may feel able to limit their operations to a relatively restricted area they know well enough to feel secure. Burglars operating in more semi-rural areas may have to become accustomed to travel greater distances. Moreover, burglars who target particular types of loot, like art or valuable antiques, will have to travel longer distances to have a sufficient choice of targets. And similarly, serial killers or rapists will operate over a larger range whose confines are determined by those areas where a large enough choice of potential targets can be found.

Marauders and commuters

Where the criminal has his own means of transport, this may give him the chance to travel a much greater distance to commit his crimes, if the abundance of targets make it attractive enough or necessary enough to do so. Professor Canter characterized the criminal who strikes out in all directions around his base as a

"marauder," while those who traveled a greater distance to reach productive targets were exhibiting "commuter" behavior. Typically, a commuter may make a single journey to reach an individual target and not follow that route again for the same reasons why a marauder would strike out in a different direction next time. On the other hand, if the commuter's journey ends in an area where there is a choice of targets, then the locations of a series of his crimes in that area will probably follow the marauder's geographical pattern, though over a more restricted area.

Peter Sutcliffe, known as the "Yorkshire Ripper," was a serial killer who struck at women over an area bounded by Manchester, Leeds and Bradford in the late 1970s and early 1980s. In this case, most of his victims were prostitutes, which largely restricted potential targets to specific areas within those three cities. His early

ABOVE: LEFT TO RIGHT
**Six of Sutcliffe's victims:
Jean Royle, Vera Millward,
Jane MacDonald, Barbara
Leach, Helga Rytka, and
Josephine Whittaker.**

LEFT
**Police and crime scene
experts find yet another
victim of the Yorkshire
Ripper.**

attacks followed a marauder pattern, but as his toll of victims extended, so did the range over which he operated. Because the geography of the area was distorted by the large empty tracts of the Pennines, the circle in which he traveled was distorted. However, an examination of the map based on choosing a base from which the total of all the distances from the base to each of the murder sites was at its minimum, placed a likely location for his base as being relatively close to Bradford. He actually lived on the northern edge of the city.

Victimology

Another way of examining the thinking and behavior of the criminal as a route to revealing his personality and background is to study the details of the victim involved. The Behavioral Science Unit of the FBI has made a point of collecting as much information as possible on the victims because of the value of this information to the profiling process. Victim details which can help profilers includes physical traits, marital status, personal lifestyle, occupation, education, medical history, criminal justice system history, and their last known activities, including a timeline of events. Other relevant information includes personal diaries, maps of their travel before the offence, their drug and alcohol history, a list of known friends and enemies, their family background, and their earlier employment history.

Physical traits are important because in the case of a serial criminal, studies of the victims' physical details can reveal whether a conscious pattern of selection governed the targets chosen. For most criminals, the gender of the victim is a powerful selection factor. Even where sex is not important in the commission of the crime, women are usually seen as more vulnerable, and therefore are targeted more frequently. In other cases, age can be important — younger targets are more attractive to a criminal predator, but in certain types of crime and for some kinds of criminal, elderly victims are seen to be less threatening and more easily intimidated targets than those of middle years.

Other details of the victims' appearance may suggest a more precise targeting process. Many serial killers attack prostitutes, either as a subject which appeals to them for reasons of revenge against women, or because they are highly accessible and not as easily missed. This victim selection can still operate even in cases where some of their victims fall outside this target profile, if their style of dress or the locations where they are found suggests they might have appeared to be prostitutes in the eyes of the criminal. Other physical attributes cause serial killers to pick victims according to a highly personal fantasy, perhaps involving length or color of hair, or whether the victims are slight or heavily built.

Marital status may well signal a vulnerability to those people closest to the victim. In some cases, an apparently amicable divorce may conceal feelings of resentment among former partners which can trigger an attack. In other cases, an apparently happy marriage can mask problems which can explode in attacks like that suffered by the wife of Sam Sheppard (*see* Case study 5, page 61). In others, the presence of young children can present a barrier to a parent seeking freedom and a new relationship, as in the case of Susan Smith (*see* Chapter 3, page 56).

Education, lifestyle, and location

The personal lifestyle of the victim may also have been an instrumental factor in bringing victim and attacker together, either directly and face to face or as the object of careful stalking and planning. Victims who belong to groups by virtue of sporting or leisure interests, or who attend educational courses, may make themselves noticeable or available to their attackers. In some cases, sudden changes in their personal lifestyle may increase their vulnerability, or even reflect an approach on the part of their eventual attacker. Occupation too can be crucial in establishing the range of people who come into contact with the victim on a regular or occasional basis, and profilers can often suggest potential suspects based on these contacts.

Educational history gives profilers another important set of networks which may have helped bring victim and attacker together. Particularly in cases of serial attacks, the educational and employment history of the victims has often been able to suggest common factors to profilers such as the network of people and places they might know in common with the other victims, which can help them narrow down the search for the criminal who targeted all the victims.

The area where a victim lives is also important to profilers. Some areas are associated with high rates of crime and therefore represent a heightened level of risk to vulnerable individuals. Mental and physical health records of the victims can also show whether their weaknesses or their behavior made them more likely as targets for their attackers. Their sexual history may also throw additional light on how their attacker may have reacted to them, and their fears and phobias may also have influenced how they came to be at risk. Moreover, changes in attitude, personality, and ways of thinking can all be important to profilers.

Finally, the victim remains the last witness of the crime, apart from the criminal himself. In cases where the victim survives the attack, their evidence can be crucial to help narrow down the search for the criminal involved. In cases where they did not survive, the best possible record of the routes and timings they followed on their way to meet their killer can be of vital importance. This would include how they traveled, what they did on the way, any witnesses who can testify as to their mood or their intentions, any phone calls or conversations, any appointments missed, and most important of all, any changes in the normal routine which made them more available and more vulnerable to their killer. All these factors can help build up a detailed and reliable picture, which can help trap the person who delivered the fatal attack.

Nathaniel Code

The One that Nearly Got Away

ABOVE
The home of Nathaniel Code in Shreveport, Louisiana, under police guard.

AS AN EXAMPLE OF A CLASSIC "marauder" killer, Nathaniel Code followed the pattern with awesome precision. All his victims were attacked and killed in the small area of Shreveport, Louisiana, where he himself lived, and one of his last victims was his uncle (originally and subsequently reported in error as being his grandfather), William Code. Nathaniel Code initially made a criminal living as a cat burglar, entering his victims' homes in darkness and making off with their possessions, though without physically attacking them.

The first break in the pattern occurred on August 31, 1984. A 25-year-old black single mother, Deborah Ford, was found dead on the floor of her living room at 315 East 74th Street in the Shreveport suburb of Cedar Grove. She was wearing a nightdress turned inside out, her wrists were bound together behind her back with electrical cord in a fashion resembling handcuffs, and she had been stabbed nine times in the chest, while her throat had also been cut no less than six times, deeply enough to cut through to her spine.

Even though the house had been burgled twice before, causing the victim's father to nail the back door shut and fix screens over all the windows, it was found the killer had managed to get in through a small bathroom window. Since Deborah Ford slept on a couch in the living room, it seemed likely that she heard the intruder and confronted him, so police wondered if this had been a case of a possible third burglary which had escalated into a sadistic killing.

With this in mind, the police started to search their records to try to find a match for the latent fingerprints they had found around the bathroom window, and the FBI was asked for a profile. They decided the killer was probably around 30 years old, lived in the immediate area and was almost certainly already on police files for crimes like rape or burglary, and would probably try to stay as close as possible to the police enquiry. At the time, the police would have had no way of knowing that as a small crowd of onlookers had gathered outside Deborah Ford's home following the discovery of her body, it had included Nathaniel Code.

The second killing was discovered a few blocks away from the first, at 213 East 72nd Street, on July 19, 1985. Here the victims were 36-year-old Vivian Chaney, her boyfriend Billy Joe Harris, her brother Jerry Culbert, and her 15-year-old daughter Carlitha. Vivian had been tied at the wrists and ankles before being led to the bathroom where she had been partly strangled and then drowned by forcing her head

underwater. Her daughter had been almost decapitated and both the men had been shot, while Billy Joe Harris had also been tied and his throat was cut.

Investigators trying to reconstruct the sequence of events decided the intruder had used the gun and the teenage girl in a hostage role as two ways of applying pressure to the other victims to do what he wanted. The girl, her mother, and Billy Joe Harris had all been tied to restrict their movements, and the killer had then shot Billy Joe Harris, muffling the gun with a pillow so as not to disturb the still sleeping Jerry Culbert. He had then shot Culbert, before cutting Carlitha's throat and forcing her mother to sit down in the pool of her daughter's blood before taking her to the bathroom and killing her. He had then returned to try to hack off Carlitha's head

BELOW
The body of Deborah Ford, the first of Nathaniel Code's victims showed a level of violence that escalated dramatically in later killings.

OPPOSITE
William Cole (right) with fellow mailroom employee Thelma Parks, pictured in 1978 – William had raised his nephew Nathaniel and was to be his final victim.

before going back to the dying Billy Joe and slitting his throat.

Apart from the horrific level of violence and the similar locality to the first crime, police found other signs to link these crimes with the earlier killing. Duct tape which had been used to gag Carlitha was the same type as that used on the first victim, Deborah Ford, and more fingerprints were found which matched those at the site of the first murder. Another link between the killings was the way in which the victims had been tied, with cords knotted in a way simulating handcuffs.

Finally, on August 5, 1987, 73-year-old William Code was found dead at his home in 641 West 66th Street in Cedar Grove. The young grandsons of a friend had been staying at the house with their mother's permission after helping William Code with some gardening the evening before. The bodies of the boys, 12-year-old Joe Robinson and 8-year-old Eric Williams, were also found in the house. Both the boys had been tied with handcuff-type bindings and also gagged, and both had suffered strangulation and massive blows to the head. The elderly man had been tied and gagged in a similar way, and

beaten about the head, but in addition, he had been stabbed seven times in the back, five times in the chest, and once in the upper arm where the knife had cut a major blood vessel.

Following these latest killings, police discovered a set of William Code's keys in a nearby drain, together with a kitchen knife. By now, other family members were beginning to speak of Nathaniel Code as a potential suspect, even though he had been brought up by his uncle in that very house. Furthermore, Nathaniel Code himself approached the police and declared he was William's nephew, in behavior which had been predicted by the FBI profilers. He also pointed out that he had been at his uncle's house earlier that morning, to explain why his fingerprints might have been found on the telephone, the vacuum cleaner, the fan, and the humidifier, all items from which cable had been taken to bind the victims. This, together with statements from relatives that Nathaniel used to beat his aunt before her death and that his uncle was reluctant to let him into the house, made the police even more suspicious. They took his fingerprints to match them to any found at the latest crime scene, and found they also matched those at the scenes of the earlier killings. More and more witnesses were able to identify him as being in the vicinity of all three crimes at around the time they were committed, and that in one case he was clearly covered in blood. Family members testified he had approached his uncle for money on the day of his murder, and that William would not give him any.

But why did the police not identify Code earlier from his existing prints in police records following his earlier arrest for aggravated rape? Unfortunately the local police were not hooked up to the nationwide computerized fingerprint records, so all prints had to be checked back manually through the paper records. It was decided, after the FBI profilers' estimate of his age, to search back over a ten-year period. Later officers would find his prints had been taken just eight months before the start of that arbitrary ten-year search limit. He was finally found guilty on December 28, 1990 of four counts of first-degree murder, and sentenced to death, though a long series of appeals on detailed points of law has followed the original verdict.

Ted Bundy

Commuter Killer Extraordinaire

WHERE MANY SERIAL KILLERS tend to target victims in the neighborhoods with which they are familiar and where they feel secure, others are able to move their scenes of operations over huge distances, setting up again in different distances in a pattern of "commuter" or "geographical-transient" crimes. Where in small countries like Britain, a commuter killer may travel a relatively short distance to commit a new series of crimes, the vast spaces of America may well result in a shift of many hundreds or even thousands of miles between one set of killings and the next, making it infinitely more difficult to track down the perpetrator.

This was very much the case for Ted Bundy, one of the most notorious of the United States' serial killers. Even while still a child, he had moved with his mother from Vermont right across the country to Washington state following his mother's remarriage, and when he graduated from Tacoma High School in 1962 he tended to roam backwards and forwards along the west coast of the U.S. He had difficulty in holding down steady jobs and occasionally broke into houses to boost his income.

He killed his first known victim in California in 1969, and moved northwards to continue killing in Oregon and Washington, before heading east to leave a trail of victims through Utah and Colorado. In essence, he was a highly organized serial killer who used a classic

ABOVE
Ted Bundy roamed from California to Florida in his search for victims and to evade arrest, a tactic which proved successful for nine years.

commuter pattern of moving on to new areas to escape detection and find new victims, and one result of his technique was that he managed to kill a dozen or so times before police discerned an apparent pattern in the disappearances of his victims or found their remains. He thought nothing of driving hundreds of miles to dump the bodies of his numerous West Coast victims at sites chosen to be inaccessible, which he could revisit time after time without their remains being found. By the time police located these sites, all that remained of many of the victims were scattered bones, often with the skulls missing as it was believed Bundy took them back home as trophies.

Bundy was very specific in targeting his potential victims, all of them young middle-class girls with small, slight frames and long hair, usually dark and parted in the middle, and conforming to a definite physical type. Because he was attracted to his ideal specification of young women, when he met 18-year-old Carol DaRonch in Salt Lake City in November 1974, he decided she fitted the prescription exactly. He told her he was a plain-clothes police officer and persuaded her to accept a lift in his Volkswagen. When he tried to handcuff her and attack her with a crowbar, she managed to escape and call the police, but her assailant had fled. Only when nine months later in the same area a police officer stopped the driver of a

"...I deserve, certainly, the most extreme punishment society has, and society deserves to be protected from me and from others like me, that's for sure."

ABOVE
Ted Bundy's high level of confidence in action, as he complains in court, while on trial for his life, about a photograph in the local Miami Herald which he said "made him out to be a villain and an idiot."

Volkswagen who had been driving without lights after dark was Ted Bundy arrested, after handcuffs and a crowbar were found in the car. Carol DaRonch identified him and he was jailed for 15 years for her attempted abduction.

Twice in the next two years, Bundy managed to escape, once from custody and, once when being taken to be charged with another murder in Colorado. After his second escape he vanished completely, to strike again in Tallahassee in the far south-east of the U.S., when he attacked and killed two young students at the University of Florida and left two others seriously injured. By now, however, his early careful planning of his crimes and the care he had taken to avoid detection had been undermined by having to be on the run for so long, and trying to operate in a new area which

was unfamiliar. After escaping from Tallahassee, he snatched his final victim, 12-year-old Kimberley Diane Leach, from her high school in broad daylight in Pensacola. He cut her throat and left her body in an abandoned pigsty some miles away, on February 9, 1978. He was finally found, drunk at the wheel of a stolen car, a week later, and arrested to be put on trial for his succession of killings.

Bundy was the subject of one of the FBI's earliest profiles. From the beginning it seemed clear they were not looking for an outwardly odd, dysfunctional loner, but someone who was attractive enough and plausible enough to tempt his young victims into his grasp. It was all too clear to the profilers they were dealing with a highly organized killer, a criminal who planned and executed his crimes so carefully and changed location so frequently that even a detailed profile was of little use in finding him and identifying him. Only later, as the net began to close around him as his identity was known, was his need to fulfil the demands of his increasing anger sufficient to overcome his organized and careful planning. Finally, this growing anger influenced his behavior, making him progressively more impulsive and more careless, to the point where the Pensacola killing eventually brought about his capture, his trial and finally his execution on January 24, 1989, after confessing to being responsible for between 40 and 50 murders in ten different states of the U.S.

Between his trial and his execution though, Bundy was able to provide the profilers with a valuable insight into how a serial killer thought, and what made him carry out his horrific crimes. Behind an outward mask of the witty, sophisticated, and clever law student, lay a violently angry person whom Bundy described as his other entity, who wanted notoriety for the killings whereas Bundy himself sought to distance himself from them. When questioned about how this other entity needed to kill innocent people and how he went about doing it, he explained a lifelong journey from a boy's preoccupation with progressively more violent thoughts to a need for violence-based pornography. This had culminated in a growing need to possess and control young women in the ultimate anger-based relationship, by killing them and keeping parts of their bodies as trophies.

Combined with this was evidence of an increasingly narcissistic personality, which developed from the police's apparent inability to catch the killer. This gave him the supreme confidence to conduct his own defense when charged with the Chi Omega murders and the Pensacola killing, despite the threat of a death sentence hanging over him. In the end though, this over-confidence was his undoing, as it succeeded in overcoming the careful, pre-planning side of his personality, striving to overcome boredom by taking greater risks, including frequently driving while drunk.

During his serial killing career, he was arrested three times for being at the wheel of his car and driving erratically in an unfamiliar neighborhood. The third time was in Pensacola, after killing Kimberley Diane Leach. He was on his way to Houston in Texas, and might well have evaded capture, had he not felt so invulnerable that he drank enough alcohol to bring him to the direct notice of the police. Yet the fact remained his careful planning had covered his tracks almost completely. The final conviction hinged on such small details as the matching of his teeth to the bite marks on the body of one of his Chi Omega victims, and the coincidence of gasoline receipts which showed he had been in the vicinity of a whole string of murders over wide areas of the U.S. at the time the killings were carried out.

LEFT
Retribution and remorse – Ted Bundy wipes away a tear while being interviewed by Dr James Dobson on the night before his execution in 1989.

CHAPTER SIX:
POWER AND ANGER

6: Power and anger

MOST OF THE CRIMES that occupy profilers' attention are those which the criminals for whom they are searching tend to repeat. These crimes are high on profilers' lists because each additional crime committed allows them to build up additional information on their quarry. Most importantly, however, the compulsion to repeat these crimes makes it especially urgent to catch the criminals responsible. The two most common categories of violent, serial criminals are serial killers and serial rapists, since these two classes of crime are triggered by appetites within the individual perpetrators which drive them to repeat the crimes in order to feed these inner compulsions.

Rape, with or without the subsequent murder of the victim, is an area of criminal activity which has provided profilers with a great deal of information about those who commit these violent attacks. In general, profilers would not get involved in two common areas of rape offences — marital rape, which some studies suggest happens at least once in as many as one marriage in seven, and the increasingly common classification of "date rape" or "acquaintance rape," where the identity of the potential offender is at least known from the beginning. Where profilers can help is in the category usually referred to as "stranger rape," where the attacker is unknown to the victim, even though the victim may be known to her attacker, in the sense of having deliberately been targeted.

Following studies of a wide range of stranger rape cases in the 1970s, the FBI began by dividing the offenders into two broad categories: selfish and pseudo-unselfish. This slightly odd-sounding classification was intended to reflect whether or not the attacker showed any consideration for his victim during the attack. In criminal terms, this reflected whether or not he tried to involve his victim in what was happening and in what ways he tried to make the act seem more like consensual sex than the rape it really was. For example, a pseudo-unselfish offender might try to kiss his victim or show a degree of tenderness toward her which quite belied what was really happening.

This has a number of important implications for the victim. Though the act is still undeniably rape, attackers of this type would tend to use the minimum force needed to subdue their victim and persuade her to submit to sex, and in some of these cases strong resistance may well persuade the attacker to back off and look for a less intimidating target. As a clue to identifying this type of personality, the language he would use would tend to be concerned, complimentary and reassuring, inquisitive and personal, and even apologetic on occasion, all intended to support his fantasy that a helpless victim is really a willing partner in what he wants to do.

The selfish rapist, on the other hand, is concerned less with intimacy than out-and-out control and sexual domination. Consequently his first and only concern is to do exactly what he wants, which produces a complete indifference for the needs, feelings, and welfare of the victim, even when compared with the pseudo-unselfish rapist. He will use much more force, probably more force than is strictly necessary, as part of the reason for his committing the act is to enjoy the sense of fear, and the physical pain, this inspires in his victim. He is likely to demand more varied and demeaning sex acts from his victim than the pseudo-

BELOW
Police in South Africa suspect a serial killer may be involved as they investigate one of four female bodies. It is a common trend for rapists to kill their victims.

unselfish rapist, who is more likely to want conventional sex as part of his normality fantasy. Furthermore, the selfish rapist will use much more threatening, abusive, and humiliating language to his victim, which reflects his need for fear and domination.

For the profiler, these distinctions are both important and useful. Victim information makes it possible to classify an attacker into one type or the other, which helps to throw more light onto what type of personality and background the attacker possesses. Broadly speaking, pseudo-unselfish rapists tend to be under-confident, while selfish rapists tends to show a much higher level of self-confidence, associated with a desire for domination over others.

Sex for sale – the kind of attraction which plays a major part in the development of power reassurance rapists.

The power-reassurance rapist

Towards the end of the 1970s, FBI profilers in the Behavioral Science Unit began working toward a more detailed system for classifying rapists. Four different types emerged which reflected the different balance between anger, power, and sexual aggression. These were:

• power-reassurance rapists
• anger-retaliation rapists
• power-assertive rapists
• anger-excitation, or sadistic rapists

Each of these types represents different danger levels to the victim, and provides different clues to profilers trying to build up an accurate, detailed, and comprehensive picture of the person responsible for a particular crime. In doing so, profilers will have to consider different types of verbal, physical, and sexual behavior to decide which type of rapist is responsible in a given case, from which they can then draw conclusions as to the type of person for whom investigators should be looking.

The power-reassurance rapist, sometimes referred to as the compensatory rapist, is the least violent of the four types. In most cases, these attackers are deeply concerned about their own masculinity. They try to compensate for this, or reassure themselves, by showing they can exercise control over their victims and force them to do what they want. However, for the deed to provide the reassurance they need, they have to be able to act out the fantasy of a sexual encounter with a willing partner. A power-reassurance rapist will often ask the victim to remove all her clothing or the minimum needed to complete the act, as part of this fantasy, and will often compliment her on her appearance and try to build up a degree of intimacy with the victim by asking her questions and giving her personal information about himself.

Providing the location is secure enough to avoid being discovered by a passer-by, the power-reassurance rapist will usually spend a considerable time with the victim, over and above that needed to complete the rape. This usually involves conversation intended to support the fantasy of intimacy and willingness between equal partners in a sexual encounter rather than the brutal and violent reality of rape. Afterwards, he may even apologize to the victim, and try to offer some kind of explanation for his conduct. In some extreme examples, power-reassurance rapists have suggested future meetings to continue what they see as a relationship, but in most cases this link is terminated with the attacker's escape from the scene. In one known case, the rapist made a promise to return to revisit his victim the following day, when he was caught by waiting police.

If the information presented to the profiler, in terms of what was done to the victim, the tenor of the conversation between attacker and victim, and the attacker's conduct before, during, and after the rape suggests he was a power-reassurance rapist, what does this mean in terms of the offender profile? It has been found that most of these criminals are single, and live with one or both parents. Their lifestyle is essentially passive with no involvement in sports or outdoor activities. They have few friends and no sexual partners. Many have minor educational problems and are likely to work in fairly menial occupations, where their passive, under-confident attitude earns them the reputation of a steady and dependable, though limited, worker. They may well spend time at so-called adult bookshops, and suffer from a number of sexual aberrations, including two in particular which may already have brought them to the notice of the police — exhibitionism, or indecent exposure; and voyeurism, or Peeping-Tom behavior which may also have resulted in victims being targeted within a relatively short distance of the offender's home.

Other facts have emerged from studying the statistics of cases involving power-reassurance rapists. In most cases the victims will be of a similar age to the rapist and from the same ethnic grouping, and will live or work within range of the offender's home or workplace for an attacker usually limited to traveling on foot. The rapes are usually committed at night, between midnight and the small hours of the following morning, and on average,

power-reassurance rapists will attack at regular intervals, every one or two weeks. In general, they will use whatever weapon comes to hand as a way of threatening the victim and persuading them to do what they want, rather than to enjoy inflicting violence as a source of pleasure. Sometimes power-reassurance rapists will cover their victim's face to assuage any feelings of guilt, and they may well take trophies from the scene or keep a diary with the details which are important to them. In most cases, these attackers will continue to rape until they are caught, and there is a danger that the amount of violence involved may escalate over successive attacks.

The power-assertive rapist

For the power-assertive rapist, the reason for the attack is less to provide reassurance of his own masculinity than a demonstration of his own macho identity through domination over his victim. This results from a belief that men are fundamentally entitled to attack women to take the pleasure they seek, though in these cases the rape itself involves aggression as well as sexual release. Consequently there is less concern for the feelings or the well-being of the victim, who is subordinated completely to the wants and preferences of the attacker.

This aggressive and self-confident masculinity shows itself in two main differences than the conduct of the power-reassurance rapist. In these attacks, the rapist will often use a degree of violence whether or not the woman tries to resist him. For example, he will typically tear off her clothing, rather than ask her to undress wholly or partially, and he may well remain with her long enough to rape her several times, with little or no sympathy for her anguish. Like the power-reassurance rapist, he will usually attack women of his own race and age group, but more frequently will time his attacks in the evening, between approximately seven o'clock and one in the morning, and will usually attack victims every 20 to 25 days. He will often rape vaginally, then anally, and then demand oral sex, and because he intends never to see his victim again, he usually makes no attempt to hide his face, nor does he usually keep souvenirs or a diary.

In terms of background, power-assertive rapists are more likely to have been brought up by a single parent or, in some cases, to have been raised in a foster home. The majority of these attackers will have suffered a degree of childhood physical abuse, and may well have dropped out of school. Their greater level of self-confidence will be reflected in a more masculine job, such as that of a building worker or even a police officer or some other occupation involving the wearing of a uniform. They will also be more conscious of their image, with a tendency towards athletic sports, and a liking for a sports car or much-modified custom car. They may well have been married more than once, though they will often be in a stable sexual relationship at the time of the attacks. In many cases they may frequent locations like singles bars, where they will find an abundance of potential victims, but they are also likely to have suffered domestic problems in the past which may have resulted in a police record for property crimes, or even a dishonorable discharge from military service.

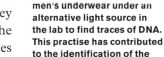

BELOW LEFT
Examining samples of semen and vaginal fluid on men's underwear under an alternative light source in the lab to find traces of DNA. This practise has contributed to the identification of the criminal in many cases.

The anger-retaliation rapist

The anger-retaliation rapist is the next classification on the ascending scale of violence and aggression. In cases involving this type of attacker, profilers look for a completely different pattern. The anger-retaliation rapist is driven by uncontrollable personal anger against dominating women in his life. In some cases the anger is caused by an over-

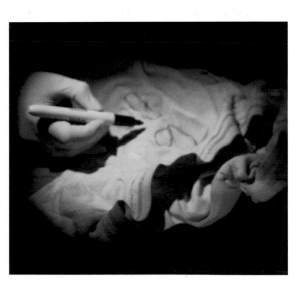

LEFT
South Side Rapist Timothy Spencer in police custody (*see* Case Study 11, page 108).

assertive mother, or a mother whom the killer assumes was responsible for a father's desertion of the family. Sometimes the mother may have been promiscuous, or a prostitute whose conduct caused the loss of the father to the family. In other cases the mother herself may have been abusive or violent, or given to specially cruel punishments in order to control her children. And in some cases, the authority figure may not be the mother at all, but a female boss or someone else with power over the perpetrator.

Very rarely does the attacker actually strike against the original source of his anger. In most cases he seeks out a victim to be punished instead, as part of his rationalized fury against womankind in general. So victims of anger-retaliatory rapists tend to have no direct link to the attacker, but nevertheless they are carefully targeted rather than just seized and assaulted as a matter of opportunity. This means there must be an indirect link — usually a geographical one — between attacker and victim. Where she lives, where she works, and how she travels between the two locations will bring her to the notice of her attacker, and suggest the opportunity for him to strike. The over-riding danger is that outside the mind of the attacker, there is nothing to identify her as his potential prey.

When the attacker finally strikes, it will usually be on ground of his own choosing and planning. In most cases, there will be an additional trigger to raise anger levels to the point where he feels he has to find and attack a victim. It may be a row with a female member of his family, a ticket from a policewoman or a female traffic warden, or even news of a woman receiving promotion, a higher salary than his, or some other distinction he sees as a threat. Another characteristic of anger-retaliatory attacks is that the attacker needs to confront his victim to push his anger over the limit from planning the crime to actually putting that plan into action. One common pattern is for him to target a prostitute and then drive her to a secluded location where he begins the argument — possibly over the prices she quotes or her refusal to perform a particular act — which will allow his anger to escalate to extreme violence.

Unlike anger-excitation, or sadistic rapists who enjoy the fear and pain they inspire and inflict on their victims, the anger-retaliation attacker tends to disable his victim with a short, sharp assault — usually a massive blow to the head, which often renders her helpless. In some cases the anger is so all-consuming that the actual rape is incomplete or unsatisfactory to the attacker, which escalates his anger to even higher levels. This often results in a frenzy of wounds being inflicted on his victim, which escalates the crime from an extremely brutal attack where the victim invariably needs hospital treatment to one of murder, even though evidence of the actual rape is partial, non-existent, or misleading.

However, once the victim is dead, his anger commonly drains away quickly. The symbolic punishment of the woman has effectively given revenge for the original provoker of his anger, and his mood will swing to the point where he sees his victim silently accusing him, provoking feelings of shame and remorse. This triggers the most characteristic behavior of this kind of killer. Because he cannot bear to have his victim seeming to watch him, he often covers her eyes with a cloth or item of clothing. Sometimes he will roll her body over on its side to avoid her stare.

Then another change of mood results. Having exhausted his anger on his hapless victim, and having escaped her accusing gaze, the killer begins to rationalize his actions on the basis that she must have deserved his anger or provoked his attack. This triggers a sense of catharsis, or emotional well-being, which can often lead to a carelessness over signs of evidence at the scene of the crime. He may take with him an item of clothing or a possession of the victim to help him relive the details of the attack, but he will then normally leave the scene soon afterwards.

What do profilers look for when they suspect a victim has been killed by an anger-retaliatory rapist? The first warning sign is a highly disordered crime scene, with large amounts of blood and repeated wounds to the victim suggesting a frenzied attack which may well show signs of having continued after her death. Sometimes the victim may have been strangled to death and her body dismembered in the violence of the attack, but in sharp relief will be the covering of the face or the victim's body being laid on her side.

If these are the signs profilers encounter, what does that tell them about the profile of the person who has committed the murder? Most anger-retaliation rapists attack women who are of a similar age to themselves or slightly older. If the victim is found to be considerably older, this might suggest a dominating, controlling mother was the original cause of the killer's anger. The killer himself will almost certainly be sociable in a superficial way rather than the classic "loner," but will have few close friends. He will probably be a keen sportsman, especially interested in contact sports like football, and may well have been married but separated from his wife.

The anger-excitation rapist

Finally, the anger-excitation, or sadistic rapist, falls into the last and most violent category of all. Here, the sexual element of the rape is merely a means to the ultimate end of inflicting physical and psychological agony on the victims. In many cases, the attitudes and behavior patterns which result in a compulsion to deliver these terrible attacks originate in childhood, with a combination of single-parent upbringing and physical — and often sexual — abuse. However, the degree of control the anger-excitation rapist wants to exert over his helpless victims is reflected in his own personal and criminal life.

BELOW
Bindings signify the degree of control which the attacker wants to exert on his victims – in this case, a woman killed by Nathaniel Code.

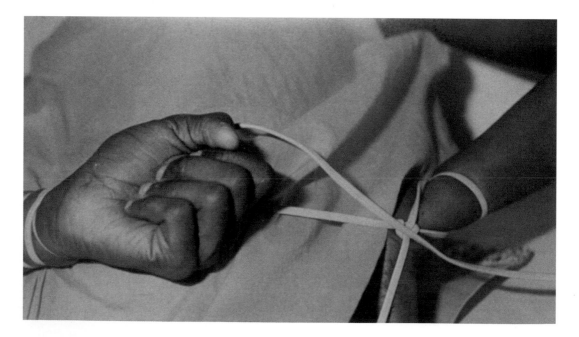

Anger-excitation rapists have a different type of personal profile from the other types of rapist mentioned above, which in many ways makes them more difficult to identify and arrest. They will typically have a middle-class lifestyle, with some college education, a white collar occupation, and an apparently stable marriage. They will usually be in their thirties, with no police record, and some evidence of compulsive behavior. Their victims' ages will vary widely, but they will usually have been carefully targeted and stalked prior to the final attack, which will be carefully planned to the last possible detail. Because this type of rapist usually has a well-maintained car, he will often attack his victim and then transport her to the chosen location for the attack to take place. There is no typical frequency to the attacks, which may well be widely separated in time from one another.

Though some of these rapists attack victims close to their own home and place of work, their careful planning and their possession of personal transport means the average distance traveled to the scene of their attacks is just over three miles. As part of the process of inflicting fear in their victims and to heighten their own pleasure, anger-excitation rapists will usually use blindfolds, gags, and other types of restraints, and will insist on telling the victim what they plans to do to her in the greatest detail and in the foulest and most intimidating language. They may also, as part of their meticulous planning, carry a "rape kit" with them consisting of weapons, restraints and other items essential to the careful sadistic fantasy which they feel it is essential to follow for maximum pleasure.

Anger-excitation rapists present two particular dangers to their victims. Apart from their utter indifference to their victims' well-being — indeed for the crime to be a success in their terms, the victim has to be harmed and terrified to the maximum degree — they may well feel the ultimate pleasure is to be had from their absolute control over the victim, by having the power to extinguish their life at any moment they choose. The other is the degree of careful planning, which makes it less likely for them to be caught, and may well, at some stage, compel them to take the logical step of realizing that the best way to prevent their victim from identifying them is to kill them once their pleasure is complete.

Timothy Spencer

The South Side Rapist

IN THE AUTUMN OF 1987, the killer who became known as the South Side Rapist murdered his first victim. In the early hours of Saturday morning, September 19, a householder living on the southern side of Richmond, Virginia, noticed a strange car was parked in front of his house with the engine running and no-one inside. The police were called, and they found the owner was 35-year-old Debbie Dudley Davis, who lived a few hundred yards away. When they called at her home, they found her body lying face-down across her bed. She had been raped and then strangled with a sock through which a length of vacuum cleaner pipe

had been twisted to produce a garrotte. The pressure applied to strangle the victim had been enough to cut into the larynx, the voice box, and the neck muscles. There was also bruising to the face, and traces of semen and internal bruising to her body, with other semen traces found on the bedding.

The killer had entered her house by lifting open a screen on a window some eight feet above the ground, by standing on a rocking chair which had been stolen from a nearby property the previous day. Almost nothing was disturbed inside, even though the killer had had to climb across the kitchen sink to reach the

floor — the only sign of a break-in was the victim's glasses and toothbrush which were found on the floor near to her bedroom door.

Victims two and three

Two weeks later, on Saturday October 3, 32-year-old neurosurgeon Dr. Susan Elizabeth Hellams was found to be the killer's second victim. Her colleagues had seen her leave for home at the end of her shift on Friday night at approximately ten minutes to eleven. Her husband arrived back at the family home, 514 West 31st Street, also on the south side of Richmond between 1.30 and 1.40 the following morning. He assumed his wife's apparent absence was due to her finishing work late, and he went straight to the bathroom to take a shower. Only afterwards did he walk into the bedroom, to find his wife's body on the floor of the walk-in closet. He called the police at four minutes to two.

The police found Dr. Hellams' body partly clothed, and lying face upwards. She had been strangled by a long ligature which still circled her neck and her hands and feet had been tied with a belt and a length of electrical cord, which the killer had found inside the house. She had been violently raped and there were traces of the killer's semen inside her body and on the nearby items of clothing. Her face was bruised, her nose broken and her right leg showed damage suggesting she had been stamped on

by her killer during the attack. He had entered by scaling a high wall around the property, and then climbed onto a porch roof to gain access to Dr. Hellams' bedroom window, where he had cut through a screen before climbing inside.

Victim number three was found just over seven weeks later. On the afternoon of Sunday November 22, the parents of fifteen-year-old Diane Cho returned home to find their daughter's body face-down on her bed, partly covered by her sheet. They had last seen her the previous evening when she had gone to her bedroom at about ten o'clock. They had later heard her typing until around eleven-thirty, but they had then gone to bed in the next-door room. They had heard nothing during the night, and when they had left for work on the Sunday morning had simply assumed that she was still asleep.

Her body was naked and her mouth sealed with duct tape. The time of death established she had been killed between two o'clock and eight o'clock that morning, almost certainly when the rest of the family had been in the house. Her killer had entered through her unlocked bedroom window after first removing the outer screen. There were bruises to the top of her head, she had been strangled with a ligature, and she too had been violently raped, with traces of the killer's semen in her body and on the bedding. There was a figure of eight sign written on her left hip in nail polish.

The fourth killing – and the killer's profile

Finally on Tuesday December 1, the body of 44-year-old Susan Tucker was found lying face-down across the bed in her Arlington home. She was naked but partially covered by a blue sleeping bag placed across her body below the waist, and she had been strangled by a rope which had also been used to tie her hands behind her back. The post-mortem determined she had died between three and five days before and that she too had been raped by her attacker. This time the killer had managed to gain entry to the property through a basement window at the back of the house.

Apart from the closeness of the four murders in terms of time and geography, there were clear signs of an identical routine followed by the killer in all four cases, which firmly established his profile as an anger-retaliation rapist. The first was the common factor in his choice of victim. All four were stockily built and similar in age, apart from Diane Cho who looked older than her years. This, together with the care taken to break into their homes, even when the family were present in adjacent rooms, showed the victims had been deliberately selected, stalked, and targeted, which suggested the killer lived in the local area. In each case, the killer had used ropes, ligatures, and duct tape to subject his victims to far more bondage than was needed to subdue them. This suggested a high level of anger against women, reinforced in one case by stamping on his victim, and by a need to control and dominate them. The figure-eight sign on Diane Cho's hip was actually the mathematical symbol for "infinity," signifying "forever" in the mind of the killer of this young virgin, who therefore believed he possessed her for all time.

Many anger-retaliatory rapists carry knives or other weapons to terrorize and mutilate their victims. In this case the killer was unusual, in using only his fists and his physical strength to overcome their resistance. Furthermore, his anger level had not reached the level where it prevented him completing the intended rapes, though further killings might have caused his rage to escalate to produce a switch from physical rape to symbolic attacks, all too likely culminating in multiple stabbings and other mutilation of the corpses after the attack.

LEFT
Halfway house, where Spencer lived in supervised accommodation as a condition of his parole for a series of burglaries, at the time when he committed the murders.

RIGHT
Comparison of DNA traces like this showed that the odds against anyone else having committed Spencer's crimes were 135 million to one.

Other indications included the way in which he posed the bodies of his victims, in differing attitudes of submission, but always partially covered up, as a means of symbolizing his exit from the scene where he had punished his victims for the anger he bore womankind. A more individual pointer was his skill at finding an entry point in each of the houses, and his skill at entering and leaving without disturbance, even when other people were present, which suggested a record as a successful cat-burglar. In addition, hairs found on the victims' bodies which were not their own had characteristics which suggested the killer was an African-American.

On the trail of the killer

Bearing in mind the localized nature of the killings, police concentrated their efforts on establishing a link between all four victims, which could account for their being seen, selected and targeted. They found it in the nearby Cloverleaf Shopping Mall, where Debbie Davis worked in a bookstore, and where Diane Cho often went shopping with her closest friend. Furthermore, Dr. Hellams had visited the bookstore on September 22, just three days after Debbie had been murdered, and less than ten days before her own death, and detectives thought it likely that Susan Tucker would also have visited the mall from time to time.

Convinced that the killer would be on the lookout for more victims, the police watched several local shopping malls, and on the evening of January 9, 1988, just over a month after the fourth murder, a recently released African-American cat-burglar named Timothy Spencer was seen to be loitering in the Chesterfield Mall watching the crowds of shoppers. After approximately an hour, he left and was followed to the Cloverleaf Mall, where he spent another half-hour standing and watching.

Eleven days later, on January 20, 1988, Spencer was arrested by the Richmond police on a charge of burglary. This allowed them to ask him for blood, saliva, and hair samples, and these were checked against the traces found at the murder scenes. Checks showed that at the time of the murders, Spencer had been living in supervised accommodation at 1500 Porter Street as a condition of his probation following

his release from prison, less than two miles from Dr. Hellams' home. Because he had to sign in and out of the home, detectives found on the night of Dr. Hellams' murder, he had left at 7.45 pm and not returned until 1.45 the following morning, having missed encountering Dr. Hellams' husband by mere minutes.

Similarly, on the night of Diane Cho's killing, he had signed out of his accommodation at 7.15 pm and did not sign in again until 8.25 the following evening. When his room was searched, an infinity sign was found daubed on the box springs of his mattress, with the words "I hope" next to it. And on the night of the final murder, Susan Tucker's, he had been given permission to leave the accommodation to visit his mother in Arlington, close to where the murder took place.

Proof positive

All this was highly significant, but the most vital evidence, once Spencer had been tracked down, was the physical evidence found at the killings. Even without the DNA evidence, the characteristics of the semen samples narrowed down the search to some thirteen percent of the population. When DNA was taken into account, the match was perfect. The chances of anyone else having the DNA profile to match the samples at the scene were estimated as being one in 135,000,000.

The importance of this case was that this had been the first one in Virginia where DNA evidence had been used to prove that an individual had committed a series of crimes. Because of the careful profiling, it was possible to convince the jury that the same person had committed all four murders, before then showing from the DNA evidence that that person was indeed Timothy Spencer. Furthermore, the combination of the killer's signature at the crime scene and the DNA evidence not only identified him as the killer of another woman in Richmond in November 1987, and a second woman in Arlington in the same November, but also brought about the release of another person awaiting execution for a murder committed in 1984, which was also believed to have been carried out by Spencer. Spencer was found guilty of all four killings and was executed in April 1994.

Paul Bernardo and Karla Homolka

The Ken and Barbie Killers

SOMETIMES IN A BIZARRE EXTENSION of the compulsion to derive pleasure from inflicting pain and humiliation on their female victims, anger-excitation, or sadistic rapists have succeeded in involving their female partners as accomplices in their crimes, usually after subjecting them to cruel and degrading behavior as their relationships developed. To all their neighbors in the upmarket area of Port Dalhousie in Ontario, Canada, Paul Bernardo and Karla Homolka seemed an attractive, clean-cut, and perfect couple. Paul was smart and well turned out and Karla was a pretty blonde. Friends nicknamed them Ken and Barbie, after the popular range of children's dolls.

Yet Paul Bernardo nursed a terrible secret. He had grown up in the working class Toronto district of Scarborough, where he had built up a record in small-time thefts and the fencing of stolen goods. In the late 1980s, there had been a series of violent rapes in the area, and the police were striving to track down the man the media were already calling the Scarborough Rapist. The sadistic rapist turned out to be Paul Bernardo. He began his career at the age of 23, on May 4, 1987, when, at one o'clock in the morning, he attacked a 23-year-old woman walking home from a bus stop. As she reached her house, he seized her from behind, flung her down on her own front lawn, and raped her vaginally and anally before beating her savagely with his fists on her face, arms, and breasts.

ABOVE
The clean-cut features of Paul Bernardo hid the terrible secrets of a classic sadistic or anger-excitation rapist.

Another attack took place on the May 13, using the same tactics. His second victim was 19-years old, and was seized on her way home from a local bus stop. This time he beat her before producing a knife to threaten her, while he fastened her wrists with restraints and tied her by the neck to her back garden fence using her belt, before subjecting her to an equally violent attack.

Love at first sight?

Five months later he met Karla Homolka, then a 17-year-old schoolgirl from St. Catherine's in Ontario, who had been visiting Toronto with a girl friend. The two girls were staying in a Howard Johnson hotel and had gone to the hotel's restaurant for a meal, where they met Bernardo and a male friend who were on the town looking for girls. In a surprisingly short time, Karla had taken Bernardo to her room for sex, as a willing partner. From December of 1987 she was seeing him regularly at weekends, and they were in constant communication by letters and phone calls. Nevertheless, Bernardo was still actively involved in his career as the Scarborough Rapist, and his attacks were growing more and more violent.

On December 16, he attacked a 15-year-old girl, at about 8.30 in the evening, again as she was walking home from a local bus stop. He raped her vaginally and anally then forced her to perform oral sex on him, after threatening her with a knife, and grabbing her hair and

LEFT TO RIGHT
Homolka's sister Tammy was drugged and raped before dying from choking on her own vomit. 15-year-old Kristen French suffered four days of abuse before being murdered. 14-year-old Lesley Mahaffie was abducted, sexually assaulted, by the couple and then strangled and dismembered.

slamming her head against the ground in a violent assault which lasted an hour. At the same time he began exerting more and more control over Karla Homolka, telling her what to wear, how to style her hair, and where she could and could not go. He began insisting on anal and oral sex, and forced her to wear a dog collar during sex, and use humiliating language which demonstrated his complete dominance over her.

During the course of 1988, as Karla was being progressively groomed for her new role as sex slave, Bernardo carried on raping women, with another five attacks by November of that year, at which point the local police called in FBI profilers Gregg McCrary and John Douglas. McCrary studied the evidence and decided that the rapist was almost certainly in his early twenties and probably living at home with his parents. He also predicted he was likely to show escalating levels of violence in subsequent attacks which would probably result in murder.

He was right on all counts. Though there was not enough detail on the original profile to identify Bernardo, an artist's impression of him was produced from witness recollections and published in local newspapers and poster outlets. In late May 1990 a woman who knew Bernardo told police the drawing looked much like him, and six months later he was taken in for questioning by police. He willingly gave samples of hair, blood, and saliva for DNA profiling, and with reasonable luck the story should have ended there and then. Almost incredibly, the Toronto Forensic Sciences Laboratory took more than two years to issue their findings, which were that Paul Bernardo was indeed the Scarborough Rapist.

Sadism turns to murder

By that time, it was too late for three of his victims. Just a month after his questioning by police, he had asked Karla Homolka for the use of her teenage younger sister Tammy as a Christmas present. By now Karla was working as a veterinary assistant, and she procured some animal anesthetic agent to drug her sister. Tammy was given a sedative in the basement of her parents' house late on Christmas Eve, and then a cloth soaked in anaesthetic was held over her nose to send her into a deep sleep. Bernardo raped Tammy and then recorded a video of Homolka sexually assaulting her helpless sister, while her parents slept unaware upstairs. Later after they left her asleep, Tammy died from choking on her own vomit, which was put down to a drink and drug-related death.

Sadly, by this time his career was progressing to still higher levels of sadistic violence. On June 15, 1991, while the laboratory was still processing his samples, he abducted 14-year-old Lesley Mahaffie and took her to the house he and Karla now shared at 57 Bayview Drive in Port Dalhousie. There they both sexually assaulted the girl, before Bernardo finally strangled her with an electrical cord and dismembered her body. The remains were partially covered in quick-drying concrete which the couple took and dumped in nearby Lake Gibson, close to Homolka's parents' home and the town of Burlington. In spite of the care they had taken, the body parts were discovered by canoeists just two weeks later, on the same

LEFT
Pictures portraying Paul Bernardo and Karla Homolka as a happily married couple hid the terrible reality.

day as Bernardo and Homolka's wedding, just a few miles away at Niagara-on-the-Lake.

Their next victim was 15-year-old Kristen French, who was abducted on the afternoon of April 16, 1992 from the car park of a church. This time the hapless girl was kept in their custody for a prolonged sexual and physical attack which lasted for a total of four days of concentrated abuse, at the end of which she too was strangled. They washed her body and then hid it in a roadside ditch not far from the cemetery where Lesley Mahaffie's body had been buried, with the intention of convincing the police that both had been the victims of a local killer from Burlington.

By then, even Karla Homolka had had enough of her violent and sadistic husband. In January 1993 she left him and went to the police to confess. Under the terms of a plea bargain, in return for giving evidence against him, she would serve two concurrent 12-year sentences for manslaughter in a psychiatric hospital rather than a prison, but the police still needed additional evidence to be sure of securing a conviction against Bernardo. Once again profilers were called in, and Gregg McCrary quoted from an FBI study of profile statistics on sadistic rapists to show it was almost certain that Bernardo would have kept detailed records of his own crimes as a way of reliving the pleasure of the attacks and killings, which he would have kept secret even from his own wife and accomplice.

Karla had told the police about Bernardo's enthusiasm for videotaping their victims, yet they knew from the profilers' advice that this information would be difficult to find. But after a detailed and painstaking search they found a set of videotapes hidden inside a light fitting in the bathroom of the couple's house at Port Dalhousie. In addition, the FBI information showed it was all too easy for someone with Bernardo's violence and readiness to threaten those close to him, to dominate a partner to the extent that Karla Homolka had apparently accepted his past as a violent rapist and the murderer of two young girls, to the point where she had even become a willing participant. However, when the details of her sentence were made public, together with her evidence at Bernardo's trial, there was a public outcry at the contrast between her relatively lenient term and the life sentence handed down by the judge at Bernardo's trial on September 1, 1995. As a result of this and other concerns, Homolka has been denied parole and is currently due to be released in 2005, at the completion of her full term of confinement, though a series of different groups on the Web claim that she will be killed soon after she leaves custody.

Dear Mom, Dad, and Lori,

This is the hardest letter I've ever had to write and you'll probably all hate me once you read it. I've kept this inside myself for so long and I just can't lie to you any more. Both Paul and I are responsible for Tammy's death. Paul was 'in love' with her and wanted to have sex with her. He wanted me to help him. He wanted me to get sleeping pills from work to drug her with. He threatened me and physically and emotionally abused me when I refused. No words I can say can make you understand what he put me through. So stupidly I agreed to do as he said. But something—maybe the combination of drugs and the food she ate that night—caused her to vomit. I tried so hard to save her. I am so sorry. But no words I can say can bring her back...I would gladly give my life for hers. I don't expect you to ever forgive me, for I will never forgive myself.

Karla—XOXO

7: Child abductors and abusers

O F ALL THE CRIMES OF VIOLENCE against the person, the one which strikes the deepest chill, especially among parents, is one involving the abduction and abuse of children. The smallest and most vulnerable of victims are open to attack from criminals who are often all too adept at maintaining a respectable and unthreatening face to society at large, and even to their intended victims until the moment they make their move. Modern criminal records and changes in legislation are intended to make the whereabouts of convicted but paroled child attackers and even murderers clear to local police in areas where they live. However, there have been many cases where the criminals themselves have managed to give their monitors the slip and gone underground, surfacing elsewhere with a new identity, to resume their activities with the advantage of additional experience to make their recapture less likely. All of which makes the help that profilers can give in identifying and directing the search for suspects even more essential.

In describing crimes against children, the terms "pedophile" and "child molester" are often used on an interchangeable basis. Yet, strictly speaking, they are quite distinct. The formal meaning of the term pedophilia refers to a tendency to harbor sexual feelings for children under the age of puberty which, while it remains an internal feeling, is not actually against the law. Pedophiles who keep their preferences to themselves, or who rationalize them through fantasy role-play with their adult partners, may actually present no direct threat to children during the whole of their lives.

Once, however, they cross the line which separates them from child molestation, they present a potentially very serious threat indeed. Child molesters, or active pedophiles, express their attraction to young children in various ways, from wanting to hold and fondle children to those who seek full sexual relations with children, and those whose inner drives lead them to seek sadistic domination over children resulting in the torture and murder of their young and helpless victims.

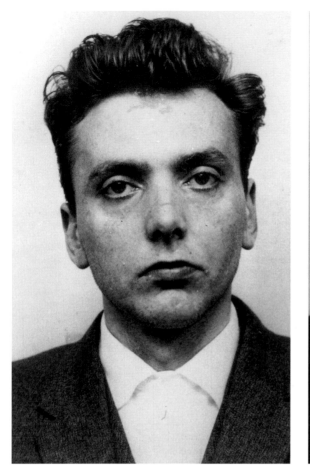

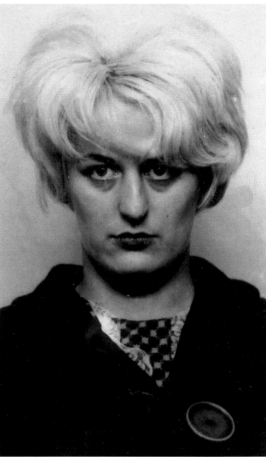

As with many other areas of criminal profiling, offenders fall into a spectrum between at one extreme, the pedophile whose preferences remain a matter of suppressed personal feelings, to the sadistic child molester and murderer at the other. However, psychologists have made it possible to recognize certain landmarks along the route between these two extremes, to help the classification of an individual and the placing of his crimes in the context of pedophile offences as a whole. At the lower end of the spectrum, there are two basic types of child molester: the situational child molester and the preferential child molester.

The situational child molester

This type of child molester will not tend to have a lifelong preoccupation with the idea of sexual relations with children, but when he meets with high-stress events in his personal life, he may well turn to this type of activity on an experimental basis, if the opportunity arises, as an alternative to molesting other highly vulnerable groups like the disabled, the ill or the elderly. To

ABOVE LEFT
Moors Murderer Ian Brady who abducted a series of child victims in and around Manchester, England, before torturing and abusing them, and burying their bodies on the high and lonely moorland of the Pennine Hills.

ABOVE
Brady's partner and accomplice Myra Hindley – opinions still differ on whether she was a willing accomplice or a reluctant participant in the series of child murders which led to her spending the rest of her life in prison.

complicate the picture further, situational child molesters can be further divided into three different types, depending on the reasons for their behavior and the nature of the threat they present to potential victims. These are:

• the regressed child molester
• the morally indiscriminate child molester
• the inadequate child molester

Regressed child molesters tend to see children as substitutes for genuine sexual partners. Indeed a regressed child molester may well have been involved in a normal adult relationship, until some key event in his life triggers a challenge to his self-esteem, like the break-up of the marriage or the loss of his job. Under these circumstances, if the heightened stress is combined with a situation which provides ready access to children, the molester may well be tempted to treat the children as sexual partners with whom he feels more comfortable. Consequently a situational child molester is more likely to abuse children he does not already know, and is also more likely to focus on girls rather than boys, where children of both sexes are available as potential targets. He is also likely to be married, with a steady job and to have lived in his current community for a long time, and may well have a secret collection of pornography with adult themes.

Morally indiscriminate child molesters have a different perspective. Like the situational child molester, the morally indiscriminate child molester probably already has an adult sexual relationship, but in this case there is no high-stress trigger to lead to the abuse of children. These criminals are sexually indiscriminate on a consistent basis, and probably have experience of unusual sexual practices like partner-swapping, voyeurism, bondage, and discipline, and children as partners merely suggest another variation to feed this need for sexual experimentation. Consequently the children abused by this type of offender may well include their own biological children or possibly step-children belonging to their current partner. He is highly likely to collect pornography, with a wide range of different subjects.

BELOW
A blurred partial frame from a CCTV recording in a shopping mall shows the two young boys just before they abducted Jamie Bulger, took him to a quiet spot beside local railway tracks, and battered him to death.

The inadequate child molester has another reason altogether for targeting children as sexual partners. In this type of offence, the normal moral mechanisms for identifying right from wrong are either missing or decayed through factors like mental illness or senility. Because of these conditions, other side effects will be apparent to neighbours or acquaintances, and these individuals will often be viewed in their communities as oddly-behaving loners who have difficulty relating to others. Consequently they find it easier to relate to children as less threatening than adults, so that they are able to strike up relationships with them.

These molesters usually form less of a physical threat to their victims. Instead of sex, they often simply crave affectionate physical contact like holding, kissing, and fondling, and their choice of victim usually depends on the friendly and non-threatening qualities they see in an individual child. This type of molester will tend to be a social misfit, probably perceived within the community as someone distinctly "odd" but not necessarily threatening. They will usually live alone or with family members, and lack other adult relationships. They may well collect pornography, but with an adult theme rather than pornography specifically featuring children.

Situational child molesters, whatever the individual type, generally present less of a threat to potential victims than the other major category, preferential child molesters.

The preferential child molester

This too is a complex classification, covering two different types of molester:

• the fixated child molester
• the mysoped child molester

The common factor in both categories which separates them from situational offenders is that they tend to *prefer* children to adults as sexual partners rather than using them as substitutes, or as experiments or because they appear less threatening than adult sexual partners. Both these types may well build up a collection of pornography, but unlike situational molesters, this will usually feature children as a consistent theme.

Fixated child molesters tend to resemble children in their behavior and lifestyle. They often appear uncomfortable in the company of adults and usually have no adult partner. Their attitude towards children is to see them as objects of affection and sexual desire, and they approach a potential victim as a normal person may conceive an affection for another person, may court them and eventually seduce them into a sexual

Wayne Williams, the Atlanta child murderer, pictured as a suspect taken in for police questioning.

relationship. In this case, the molester knows the victim, and often works slowly to build up a relationship through buying gifts and sharing interests with a potential victim until a physical relationship develops.

Though this still represents abuse, the victim is not generally in real physical danger from the molester, who feels great affection for children. The sexual relationship will usually involve oral sex to begin with, and only later develop into full sexual intercourse after a relatively long time. Though victims are predominantly boys, the majority of these molesters are actually heterosexual in preferences.

Mysoped, or sadistic child molesters have a completely different attitude to their victims. Here the driving force is a need to inflict personal violence on the child and cause them harm. These molesters usually do not know their victims, but stalk likely prospects until they can seize the opportunity for abduction. They commonly target locations like schools, playgrounds, shopping malls, and other public places, where their approach and abduction of their victims is less likely to be noticed in the crowds. Often they simply take the child by overwhelming physical force. The attraction the victim possesses for this type of violent criminal is his or her vulnerability and helplessness, and once the child is in his power the molester usually inflicts severe physical harm on the child, often to the point of death and beyond. Often the victim's body is mutilated after death, with a minority of molesters actually cannibalizing parts of their victims.

These individuals tend to have an antisocial personality, and may well have an existing criminal record for offences like rape, assault, and other violent acts. They may well have moved from one address to another over a long succession, with short-term jobs, and commonly move on after committing an abduction or murder. If they have a collection of child pornography, this will normally feature a theme of brutality, violence, and sadism.

FBI profiler Roy Hazelwood has drawn attention to a large number of similarities between mysoped child molesters and sadistic killers of adult victims. Both types tend to ascribe a high level of fantasy and ritual to their crimes, so that the bodies of their victims are often treated according to a particular script which varies from one individual criminal to another, but tends to remain constant for that individual. Both types of criminal are highly motivated to commit their crimes, because of the high level of personal satisfaction they derive from the violence they inflict on their victims.

Additionally both types are able to rationalize their behavior so they can feel comfortable with what they do, and neither feels any guilt or remorse on account of the acts they commit. They feel outcasts from conventional society, and may well have been abused in childhood. They tend to be vain, suffer easily from sexual boredom, and record their acts in some way which allows them to relive them afterwards. They are likely to abuse their own children, and, if caught, are able to play by the rules sufficiently to be regarded as model prisoners, and as prime candidates for parole. Finally, and most disturbingly of all, both types have extremely low rates of reform, and will commonly continue to find and abuse victims until well into old age.

Wayne Williams

The Atlanta Child Murderer

ONE OF THE EARLIEST HIGH-PROFILE child murder cases to involve the FBI's Behavioral Science Unit was triggered by the discovery on July 28, 1979 of the body of two male black teenagers in the undergrowth which bordered Niskey Lake Road in the south-eastern part of the city of Atlanta. The first victim was revealed to be 14-year-old Teddy Smith, who had been missing for a week, and who had apparently been strangled. The second victim, lying some 50 feet away, was 13-year-old Alfred Evans who had been missing just three days, and he had been killed with a .22 caliber bullet.

Police tried to establish a link between the two victims, and found they were former schoolmates. Although they no longer lived close to one another, it was established they had both been seen at a partly shortly before their deaths, and this appeared at first to be a potentially hopeful link. Before long, however, the hope was shown to be an illusion as the bodies of more and more victims, with widely differing backgrounds, were discovered in frighteningly quick succession.

On November 8, a passer-by found the body of 8-year-old Yusef Bell, missing since going on an errand to local shops on October 22, in a hole in the concrete floor of an abandoned school. Victim number four was 14-year-old Milton Harvey, missing since early September, and by June the following year the total of black children found murdered in the Atlanta area amounted to eight boys and two girls.

At that stage there was no positive evidence to confirm that all these murders had been committed by the same person, and local speculation produced rumors of everything from a serial killer, to sinister Government agencies, and the hand of the Ku Klux Klan. The police lacked any positive leads, and FBI profilers Roy Hazelwood and John Douglas were called in to examine the findings. By this

time, six more victims had been found, with no positive link except that all of them were black. Some had been seized while outside, one had been abducted from her bedroom, and another had been the focus of an extortion attempt which suggested he had been taken to Alabama and that a ransom would see him returned to his parents.

White – or black?

Along with the lunatic-fringe theories of U.S. Government involvement, the profilers rejected the idea of Ku Klux Klan or Nazi party involvement, as a series of political crimes against the black community — they reasoned that any action of this type would result in the killings being widely publicized as highly visible and symbolic acts. Were they the work of a serial killer? The majority of serial killers are white, but this was unlikely in this case for two reasons: serial killers usually target victims from their own racial group, and the bodies had been dumped in predominantly black areas where a white face would have been seen, and remarked upon, by witnesses.

The profilers suspected that most of the murders were the work of a single killer who was almost certainly black. Most of the victims were young enough to be streetwise, but naïve about the world outside their own neighborhood, and were likely to have been persuaded to venture within the power of a plausible pedophile until it was too late to escape. They were less confident about the killings of the two girls, including the one abducted from her bedroom, and about the victims who had not been strangled. In one

OPPOSITE
Atlanta child killer Wayne Williams after being arrested and charged with the murder of two of his list of victims.

BELOW
The Chatahoochee National Forest in Georgia provided Williams with a choice of secluded disposal sites for the bodies of his many victims.

or two cases, there were strong indications the killings had been carried out by members of the victim's own families, but the profilers were clear that the majority of the murders were still down to a single individual.

They drew up an initial profile. They saw the killer as a black male, aged between 25 and 29, who, like many serial killers, would have a keen interest in police matters. Accordingly, they suspected he might drive a make and model of car commonly used by the police and that he might well have a dog of a breed used by the police, like a Doberman or German Shepherd which FBI files show is another common factor among serial killers preying on these younger and more vulnerable victims. They also concluded he was not married, and was sexually attracted to the young male victims, even though there was no evidence of their having been sexually assaulted. They deduced he was sexually inadequate, and must have some routine which persuaded the victims to trust him. In a moment of inspiration, they suggested he might pretend to have some connection with the musical world, but that when his targeted victims realized he was bogus, they would withdraw from the relationship, which triggered him into killing them.

Outwitting the killer

Unfortunately the publicity created by the idea of a serial killer at large in the community set off a number of false leads, including the arrest of suspects who proved to have no connection with the crimes, and a number of hoax calls from a man claiming to be the killer, who sneered at the police for not catching him. Finally, in a landmark in profiling history, John Douglas realized that the almost obsessive interest of the press was actually producing a response from the killer. One press report revealed that, following a call from the person who later turned out to be an impostor, the police had searched a route called Sigmon Road for another body, but in vain. Soon afterwards, the body of another victim was found along the stretch of road covered by the fruitless police search, and the profilers concluded their quarry was following the press coverage very closely.

The next significant fact revealed by the press — from a leak within the medical examiner's office — was that forensic examinations had

found that hair and fibers found on the body of the latest victim matched those found at five of the earlier murders. Douglas realized that if the attacker heard these details, he would take extra care to ensure the bodies of his next victims would be free of this potentially incriminating evidence. In other words, he would probably start dumping his victims in the river, and it was time to start patrolling likely stretches of the local waterways.

Douglas was right. The next victim was found in the South River, and later two more turned up in the Chattahoochee River on the north-western side of the city. All three bodies had been stripped of their outer clothing to ensure all traces of hair or fibers had been washed away by the river. A major surveillance operation was mounted, but limited funds meant that it would be closed down at six o'clock in the morning of May 22, 1981 if nothing was found. With just three and a half hours to go, a police patrol reported hearing a splash below the Jackson Parkway bridge over the Chattahoochee river, where a car had stopped in the middle of the span. The car drove off, turned round, and then came back across the bridge. Police stopped it, and found the driver was Wayne Williams, a 23-year-old black man who claimed to be a music promoter. He lived with his parents, he owned a German Shepherd dog, and had previously been charged with impersonating a police officer. He had also previously owned a former police car, and had used a police scanner to enable him to visit and photograph crime scenes.

The mysterious splash which had caught the officer's attention was explained two days later when the naked body of 27-year-old Nathaniel Cater surfaced not far from the bridge. Wayne Williams was arrested and his car examined in meticulous detail. The fibers found on the earlier victims were traced to those of a carpet in Williams' parents' house and in the trunk of his estate car, and the hairs to his dog. Williams was arrested and charged with the murders. Though he remained contemptuous of the police to the last and refused to admit to any of the killings, he was finally found guilty of the murder of Nathaniel Cater and of 21-year-old Jimmy Ray Payne, as these two victims — though outside the age range of the rest of his victims — showed the best evidential links to their killer. On February 27, 1982, Wayne Williams was given two life sentences.

OPPOSITE
Nathaniel Cater was, at 28, both the oldest and the last of Wayne Williams' victims – as he was disposing of Cater's body, police heard the splash and arrested the killer.

BELOW
Williams' home in West Atlanta – as Douglas had predicted, the killer still lived at home with his parents.

Julie Kelley

Abbie Humphries' Abductor

FORTUNATELY NOT ALL CHILD ABDUCTIONS, though harrowing for the parents, actually threaten the child's life. Abbie Humphries, the daughter of Roger and Karen Humphries, was abducted from the Queen's Medical Centre hospital in Nottingham, England, hours after her birth on July 1, 1994. While Abbie's mother was out of the room telephoning her mother with news of the birth, and Abbie was with her father and three-year-old brother, a woman wearing a nurse's uniform had come to take the baby for a hearing test. When Karen arrived back minutes later and heard where Abbie had been taken, she was immediately suspicious. As a midwife, she knew that babies were not normally given hearing tests within hours of their birth, and the alarm was raised. Witnesses and CCTV footage revealed that the woman had changed into civilian clothes and left the hospital, with Abbie in her arms.

This was the cue for a massive police operation, but first of all it was essential to try to determine what kind of person had taken the baby and what kind of threat she represented to the baby's well-being. Psychologist and profiler Paul Britton was called in to advise the police, and he explained that the woman was probably aged between 20 and her early 30s, and the evidence of witnesses showed that she was comfortable in a hospital setting where the part she was playing demanded she appear confident and in authority. She must also have had a reasonably good standard of education, since the abduction involved a degree of advanced planning, including acquiring a false uniform and a wig which had been used for disguise and then discarded along with the uniform in the transformation back to an anonymous civilian.

She also had the confidence to talk to the father of the baby, and respond to any

objections being placed in her way, which meant she was a skilled deceiver. On the other hand, when she was making her escape from the hospital, she seemed to show a sense of panic, and it was likely that she had only planned the actual abduction in detail, but had not thought the matter through to the extent of bringing clothes or blankets for the baby. Nevertheless, Britton was sure that her home setting would be completely prepared for a new baby, including the creation of a cover story to account for its arrival.

Why abduct a baby?

Britton also concluded she was married or in a long-term relationship, which might well be under strain to the point where she might feel producing a baby would solve the problem. This was his conclusion after rejecting the idea that she might be mentally ill, and convinced the baby was genuinely hers, or that she might be isolated and unable to form relationships with adults, abducting a baby as a substitute.

Other possibilities which were rejected included the hypothesis that the woman had a specific grudge against the parents. It transpired that mother and baby had originally been meant to be in a different ward, and had been moved at short notice, which the abductor could not possibly have known. A grudge against the hospital would probably have triggered a different kind of action which would not directly threaten such a young life, or the world of innocent people outside the hospital organisation.

If the profile was correct, Abbie was in little immediate danger. The first priority was to rescue her before the abductor formed a deep enough bond with the baby to reject any persuasion to return her, and the second was the need to avoid panicking the abductor into abandoning the baby while she was still so vulnerable. A careful campaign was put in train to appeal to the abductor herself and stress the strain imposed on Abbie's parents, and later to widen the focus to include those who were likely to know the abductor. Unfortunately this careful approach was threatened by internal police politics resulting in sensitive information being released to the media, and the enquiry was plagued by hoax calls and false leads.

Success at last

Ultimately, though, the campaign was entirely successful. Among a total of 4,700 calls received from the public by the police were

ABOVE
Abductor Julie Kelley on her release from hospital a year later – she had taken the baby to support her attempt to rescue a failing relationship by claiming to be pregnant.

several relating to a house in the Nottingham suburb of Wollaton, where 23-year-old Leigh Gilbert, a motor mechanic, lived with his mother and his long-term girlfriend Julie Kelley, a 22-year-old former dental nurse. When police followed up the calls, they found a family apparently celebrating a new baby with no sign whatsoever of anything wrong, and they crossed them off their list. Nevertheless, calls still pointed to the household, and when a midwife eventually checked the official records, she found there was no trace of a home birth at that address.

The police returned, retrieved Abbie who was in perfect health, and arrested all three. Julie Kelley admitted abducting Abbie two weeks earlier, and claimed she had done it to repair her foundering relationship with Gilbert, who had already met someone else. She had claimed to be pregnant, had had a spare room decorated as a nursery, and had bought a pram and other baby equipment. She managed to dupe both her boyfriend and mother-in-law by playing the perfect part: she wore padded clothes as the

pregnancy appeared to develop, complained bitterly of morning sickness and food cravings, and even went to the Queen's Medical Centre for ante-natal appointments, though always made her boyfriend wait in reception while she pretended to see a doctor. In an unexpected twist of fate, she became genuinely pregnant two months before the abduction, but by then the deception was too far advanced for her to tell the truth. Finally, she had made the abduction while her boyfriend and his mother were out of the house, wearing the uniform she had used as a dental nurse, and told them later she had given birth suddenly while they were away.

8: Kidnapping and extortion

PROFILING HAS BECOME VITALLY IMPORTANT in another area of criminal activity where an insight into the thinking, attitudes, and likely behavior of the criminals is of immeasurable value. The closely allied crimes of kidnapping, or seizing a hostage to force the payment of a ransom, and extortion, where a criminal threatens to carry out a crime like the contamination of food unless a manufacturer or a store chain meets their demands, have involved the efforts of profilers to identify the background and personality types of the people involved, as an aid to outwitting them and helping to track them down and ultimately identify them. This is another area of criminal activity where the perpetrators are commonly men. Although poisoning is a method often favored by female killers, these usually target specific individuals, like family members or work colleagues, against whom the poisoner may have a personal grudge. Threatening to poison anonymous victims as a means of gaining a ransom is still mostly a male activity.

The greatest difference between profiling this type of crime and profiling crimes of violence is the channel of communication between criminal and profiler. In these cases, the classic crime scene as an indicator of the criminal's drives, motives, personality, and methods of thinking is replaced by the notes, telephone messages, and other interaction between the criminal and his targets, and between the criminal and those seeking to identify and track down the criminal and his helpers. Not only do these provide vital insights which help to build up a psychological profile of the criminal behind the plot, but they constitute vital evidence in themselves, once the perpetrator has been caught and put on trial. For reasons like this, FBI profiler John Douglas advised bank staff that when a robber passed them a hold-up demand note across the counter, they should on no account hand it back. Instead, they should feign panic and contrive to drop it on the floor while appearing to accede to his demands. This made it likely the note would be overlooked by the criminal and would remain behind even if the robbery was successful, whereupon it could be examined and analyzed for any clues it might reveal.

In many kidnapping cases, the criminal involved is a variation on the familiar serial-killer or serial-rapist types. Where these individuals derive their intense personal satisfaction from the degree of control they exert over their terrified victims, up to and including the power of life and death, violent kidnappers want to extend that control to the families and loved ones of their victims as well. By appearing to open negotiations for a ransom demand and setting up elaborate schemes for the collection of the money and the return of the victim to the family, they can inspire and maintain a degree of hope among the extended group of their victims, when all too often the original victim is already dead.

Only in cases where the kidnap attempt is a genuine attempt to extort money does the criminal have a vested interest in returning the victim safely once the money had been collected. However, here too there are powerful incentives to kill the victim. In the first place, the collection of the ransom is the moment of maximum danger, when they are likely to be identified and caught, and even if this should prove successful, there is always the danger the liberated victim may remember some detail which may reveal their identities to the police.

BELOW
Police artist's sketch of the man believed to be responsible for the kidnap of Stephanie Slater, from witnesses who had seen him waiting outside her workplace (*see* Case Study 15, pages 142-146).

Checking the communications

For reasons like these, profilers examine very carefully the nature of the communications made by the kidnappers. Suggestions that the victim will be returned without a detailed and credible ransom demand are immediately suspect — in that case, why abduct the victim in the first place? If a ransom demand has been made, does it suggest the kidnappers have done their planning sensibly? Is the sum of money demanded large enough to justify the enormous risk of taking a hostage, and does it bear any relation to the kind of sum the family are likely to be able to lay their hands on at the shortest of notice? Does it appear that the victim was chosen on the relative wealth of his or her family, or merely on the relative accessibility of the victim as a target for abduction? And finally, was the ransom demand made as quickly as possible after the seizure of the victim? Genuine kidnappers want to minimize the length of time they hold their victim, because of the danger of identification or capture, and also to help them retain the initiative over the forces being assembled to catch them.

ABOVE
British turkey farmer Bernard Matthews was the victim of an ingenious extortion attempt, which Rodney Whitchelo used as the basis of his attack on the manufacturers of Heinz Baby Food (see Case Study 17, page 150).

For the kidnapper, this type of crime is an extremely high-risk means of forcing the payment of a ransom. Every stage of the operation, from targeting a potential hostage of a well-off family to identifying a suitable spot to carry out the abduction, from finding a suitable safe house and determining a safe and anonymous channel of communication, to collecting the ransom and returning the victim unharmed, is fraught with the danger of the criminals themselves being identified, caught, and punished, usually with a very long prison sentence.

Compared with the clear and proven risks of kidnapping, for many criminals the alternative of corporate blackmail crimes seems to offer an equally effective route to a ransom, without the additional dangers of a human hostage. Instead, the criminal merely has to make a credible threat to poison or contaminate food or medicinal products on the shelves of a supermarket or pharmacy, and the theory is that the company which makes the products or runs the retail outlets will pay to avoid the inevitable bad publicity and flood of expensive compensation claims. On the face of it, this is a much less dangerous crime to commit. Assuming the need to convince the targets for the extortion attempt that the threat is serious, all the criminal has to do is place examples of the contaminated products on the shelf of any branch of the targeted store chain. Instead of the few wealthy potential victims to provide the kidnapper with the desired ransom, there may be hundreds or even thousands of stores open to the criminal with a jar of contaminated baby food or painkillers spiked with poison.

When profilers began to examine the motives and attitudes of criminals involved in product tampering cases, they found a consistent pattern in that the most powerful motive in the majority of cases was anger. This would be a result of a real or imagined grievance against the makers of the product, the store chain where it was sold, or society in general. The criminal involved would tend to have a long history of failures in many different areas of life, including education, employment, social life, and relationships. He would have difficulty meeting women of his own age groups and levels of intelligence, and may well also suffer from physical disabilities, ailments, and limitations.

Another common factor among people with this type of profile is a tendency to gravitate towards jobs with some connection to authority, like security guards, auxiliary firefighters or ambulance drivers, though in keeping with the pattern of failure, there may well have been problems in keeping these jobs. In some cases, the individual may well have served in the military, particularly in the less technical branches like the Army or the Marines, but here too there would usually be evidence of behavioral problems and possibly a record of psychiatric treatment.

The Tylenol murders

Perhaps the classic product tampering case in the U.S. was the Tylenol murders in the Chicago area in the autumn of 1982. It was unusual in that it failed to follow the usual pattern of these extortions, whereby the criminal responsible succeeds in contaminating some vulnerable product, places it on the shelves of a store, and then delivers the threat by alerting the authorities anonymously to tell them what he has done. The message is simple — he is telling them he has done this once without being stopped or identified, and given them a warning to allow them to take the contaminated products off the shelf. Unless they give him what he wants, he will repeat the operation without warning, resulting in possible death or injuries to innocent customers.

In the Tylenol case, the criminal delivered his threat in a much more chilling and lethal form. He took packages of a common non-prescription painkiller called Tylenol Extra Strength and laced the tablets they contained with a lethal poison — potassium

BELOW
The Tylenol Extra Strength painkiller capsules which were opened, contaminated with potassium cyanide, and resealed with no outward signs of having been tampered with.

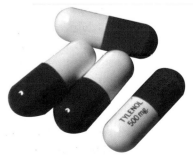

Much more serious, however, was a letter from someone who signed himself "Robert Richardson." This demanded a ransom of $1 million, to be paid into a Chicago bank account, otherwise future poisonings would be carried out. He boasted that each contamination drop took him less than 10 minutes to carry out and so far the whole operation had cost him less than $50. A series of other letters from the same source was received by newspapers in Chicago and Kansas City, denying any connection to the poisonings, and demanding the police reopen an investigation into the 1978 murder of Raymond West.

These letters were postmarked New York City and this gave Douglas a new means of catching his quarry. He knew that out-of-town criminals often kept in touch with what was happening at home through reading up their local papers at major public libraries which kept a wide range of newspapers in their reference departments. New York police and FBI agents watched the main libraries for anyone studying Chicago papers who matched the descriptions or CCTV footage from drugstores which may show the poisoner making his calls.

On December 12, 1982, they caught their man. He turned out to be a 36-year-old former Chicago accountant, James William Lewis, who had used the Robert Richardson alias two weeks after the poisonings, when writing to President Reagan to threaten to assassinate him if certain taxation policies were not changed according to the writer's demands. His connection with the Raymond West case, which was the subject of his earlier letter to the newspapers, is that murder victim Raymond West was a former client of his accountancy practice, and the police believed that he had been poisoned, though the cause of death could not be determined positively. From the text of the letter, Lewis clearly felt that suspicion was directed at him, which he blamed on a half-hearted police investigation. Though married, he fitted the resentful loner profile in many other respects, especially in terms of writing threatening letters to public figures and mentioning the investigation into the death of his former client. Additionally, the language used in his letters too accorded with Douglas' profile, where he described this type of criminal as unable to contemplate direct, face-to-face contact with his targets, therefore unlikely to carry a weapon, preferring instead to kill random victims in an impersonal way.

BELOW
Opportunist criminal Vernon Williams, who was jailed for sending ransom demands to the makers of Tylenol, even though he had no connection with the actual poisonings.

In the end, Lewis was never charged with the Tylenol murders because police were unable to prove he had carried out the actual contamination of the tablets. He was, however, tried and jailed for 20 years for the extortion. Nevertheless, most of those who hunted him down were adamant he fitted the profile so precisely that they remain convinced he was the Tylenol poisoner. Whether or not they are right, with his arrest the poisonings stopped. In addition, he explained to a newspaper reporter in an interview while in prison how the contamination "might actually have been carried out" even though he claimed not to have done it himself, a classic and common defence mechanism among criminals involved in the deaths of others.

ABOVE
James William Lewis who was tried and convicted for the extortion campaign against Tylenol's manufacturers, though police failed to prove he had actually carried out the contamination of the tablets.

Coping with future cases

Huge sums of money were spent in changing the packaging of all kinds of foods and medicines to make it difficult or impossible to tamper with them without the fact being obvious. Another consequence of the Tylenol poisonings is that profilers now look much more closely at the notes which arrive in similar cases threatening that the criminal is about to do these terrible things unless a ransom is paid. Words and phrases are analyzed to determine the relative probabilities of the writer being someone capable and willing to carry out the crime or merely a fantasist seeking to exert a sense of power. Secondly, they look at the details given for the actual payment of the money — does this reveal the fact that the criminal has thought through the method of delivery, to enable him to pick up the cash with a reasonable prospect of evading capture, or does it show a naïve and ineffectual scheme which would inevitably result in him being caught red-handed?

Other clues in the written or telephoned communications include the amount of ransom demanded — is the target able to deliver that kind of sum within the time given? When is the demand made? Large amounts of cash cannot easily be raised over a weekend, which might point to a criminal who has little or no experience of financial institutions and how they operate.

Finally, another possibility is that a criminal might use a false case of product tampering to deflect attention from their own activities. On June 11, 1986, 40-year-old Susan Snow, a newly remarried bank employee living on the outskirts of Seattle, was found dead on her bathroom floor with symptoms of cyanide poisoning shortly after taking some extra-strength Excedrin painkillers. Checks cleared her family of any suspicion of involvement in her death. However, almost a week later, Stella Nickell called the Seattle police to report that her husband, Bruce Nickell, who had apparently died from emphysema two weeks before, had also taken extra-strength Excedrin painkillers shortly prior to his death. She then announced her intention to sue the manufacturers, Bristol-Myers, in a wrongful-death action for compensation.

Product tampering — or insurance fraud?

So far, it seemed to be another classic product tampering case. However, when police checked the overall pattern of poisonings, they discovered a grand total of five bottles containing cyanide in all the stores they checked. Of the five, two were found in the Nickell home, but Stella Nickell claimed she had bought the bottles from different stores at different times. The chances of two contaminated bottles out of five being bought by the same person out of the vast number of uncontaminated bottles were truly astronomical, and the police began looking more closely at the Nickell family.

Traces of other chemicals were found in the contaminated tablets – chemicals which were present in a particular type of algae exterminator used by owners of tropical fish. The police concluded the poisoner had used the same container for the

LEFT
Paul Webking, holding a picture of his late wife, Susan Snow, who was inadvertently killed by the Excedrin painkillers Stella Nickell laced with cyanide in order to kill her husband.

cyanide as had earlier been used for the algicide, which is how the cross-contamination occurred. The Nickells kept tropical fish, and an assistant at one pet store recalled Stella Nickell ordering the algicide together with a pestle and mortar to grind up tablets into powder. They also found large insurance policies on the life of Bruce Nickell with Stella Nickell as the beneficiary, several of which were endorsed by a forgery of Bruce's signature. They also found she had a record of forgery, check fraud, and child abuse, and that she was facing bankruptcy proceedings at the time of her husband's death, circumstances which would have been drastically transformed by large compensation payouts from the manufacturers of the painkillers and under the terms of the insurance policies.

On May 9, 1988, Stella Nickell was found guilty of murder and sentenced to two terms of ninety years apiece, one for murdering her husband and the other for killing Susan Snow, together with three terms of ten years apiece for the product tampering. She was the first person in the U.S. to be convicted of murder through product tampering, and Snow was her entirely innocent victim. Susan Snow's role was to provide a cover story for Stella Nickell's ingenious but ultimately unsuccessful insurance fraud.

Michael Sams

Kidnap Escalates to Murder

EIGHTEEN-YEAR-OLD JULIE DART lived with her mother in Leeds, England, but often stayed at her boyfriend, Dominic Ray's apartment. On July 7, 1992, she and Dominic had a violent row which resulted in both of them turning up early in the morning at the casualty department of St. James' Hospital for treatment for their injuries. Julie had head and facial wounds, and Dominic a broken ankle. The couple discharged themselves from hospital later in the day, and on the evening of July 9, Julie left for work as a laboratory assistant at the Leeds General Infirmary, where she worked several nights each week.

She never returned. Three days later a note was delivered to Dominic's apartment which appeared to be in Julie's handwriting, saying that she had been kidnapped and telling her mother to contact the police. No mention was made of any ransom demand, but on the same day a long, typewritten letter arrived at Leeds police headquarters referring to the kidnapping of "a young prostitute" from the Chapeltown area of the city and threatening to kill the hostage and fire-bomb a city department store unless a ransom of £150,000 was paid under strictly specified conditions. These included the placing of two separate £5,000 payments in different bank accounts with cash cards and PIN numbers provided, and the requirement for a woman police constable to deliver the remainder of the cash on Tuesday, July 16, wearing a "lightish blue skirt" and carrying the money in a shoulder bag.

The first of many detailed instructions came from a number of public telephone booths where the woman police constable (WPC) would receive detailed instructions to drive down a succession of quiet country lanes where any additional traffic could be spotted. The details for the dropping off of the ransom were carefully planned, and the kidnapper revealed

ABOVE
Teenager Julie Dart, who was Michael Sams' first kidnap victim, but who was murdered as negotiations for her freedom were actually in progress.

the ransom would be picked up by a male individual acting under duress as his partner, too, had been kidnapped by the criminal responsible for the whole exercise.

On the appointed day the telephone in the first telephone booth rang as promised. The WPC answered it, but no-one spoke at the other end. No further call was received and three days later Julie's body was found wrapped in a sheet lying at the foot of a tree close to the A1 trunk road and a disused railway line. She did not appear to have been sexually assaulted, and had been killed by two heavy blows to the back of the head which had fractured her skull. The autopsy revealed she had been dead for at least a week, and was therefore almost certainly dead when the two letters had been delivered.

When police made enquiries at Leeds General Infirmary, they were amazed to find no-one there knew her, and her job did not in fact exist. She was, however, known under several false names as a part-time prostitute in the Chapeltown red-light district (though both her family and boyfriend strongly denied she had had any connection with prostitution), and several women confirmed she had been working there on the night of her disappearance.

Profiler Paul Britton was called in by Leeds police to draw up a blueprint for the kidnapper to help them know what kind of person they were looking for. The only clues were contained in the two letters, and his first conclusion was that the long and detailed letter sent to the police was planned and written before the kidnapping, while the other was clearly dictated to Julie after her abduction. Next, he assumed that the kidnapper had targeted a prostitute as an ideal hostage, since she would be easier to approach and would more than likely trigger

treat him with respect because of his audacity and his meticulous planning. On the other hand, cutting off the ransom arrangements at the first phone call, together with Julie's murder were probably carried out deliberately and cold-bloodedly, to prove to the police the kidnapper was in deadly earnest, and should be taken very seriously indeed when he next made a demand.

Britton also concluded, from the language, spelling, and grammatical errors in the letters, that the kidnapper was in his late 40s or early 50s, educated to secondary school rather than university level, and with a knowledge of electrics and machinery. He was also likely to have a police record for lower-level offences like fraud and deception, and might well have a personal or family grievance against the former Leeds City Police, to which his letter had been addressed though that force had ceased to exist.

Over the following four months police received a succession of letters and threats from the kidnapper. In one he claimed to have abducted another prostitute, though no-one was found to be missing, and in another he threatened to derail a crowded express train at high speed. The police were beginning to suspect the whole exercise was developing

> "Don't ask me why, I've no idea why I did it. Stephanie would never have been killed. She was terrified. It was the first time in my life that anybody's been frightened of me. I always had dominating women in my life, I've always accepted that but didn't like it." Michael Sams about the Julie Dart killing

less immediate alarm bells if she failed to return home on schedule.

The one point which seemed illogical was the direct involvement of the police from the beginning. Britton's conclusion was that the primary motive of the kidnapper was not the money, since the sum demanded was relatively modest in relation to the amount of effort and risk involved. Instead, he decided, this was much more a case of a direct challenge to the police, and a demand that they should come to

into a game which allowed the kidnapper to taunt them with impunity, and they began to scale down their responses, refusing to play the kidnapper's game by missing phone calls and ignoring instructions.

The kidnapper struck again some six months later on January 22, 1993, when Stephanie Slater, a 22-year-old estate agent, had left the branch office in the Great Barr district of Birmingham to show a client round a vacant property. She failed to return and two days later, the kidnapper called her office and told the staff they would receive a random demand the following day. When police retrieved the note they found another detailed set of demands, this time written on a word processor, and with several differences than the Julie Dart kidnapping. The note warned Kevin Watts, the estate agency manager, (who from the wording of the letter had originally been intended to be the hostage) not to contact the police under any circumstances. The kidnapper had also taken the risk of being seen while waiting for Stephanie to turn up at the vacant property, and witnesses had been able to produce a sketchy description. Finally, he had sent corroboration that he held Stephanie, not in the form of a letter in her own handwriting, but on an audio cassette with her reading from a prepared script.

Once again Paul Britton studied the wording of the letter in great detail and decided, in spite of the shift from Leeds to Birmingham and the different arrangements for providing the ransom money, that this was almost certainly from the kidnapper and killer of Julie Dart. In the meantime, Stephanie's family had received an audiotape through the post in which she referred to the result of a local football match as proof she was still alive.

The police complied with the kidnapper's instructions. Kevin Watts was given the ransom money provided by Stephanie's employers and provided with a two-way radio to communicate with police cars following at a distance. On the evening of January 29, he was ordered to drive all the way to a railway station at Glossop to the east of Manchester. Directed to telephone booths for further instructions, he was steered by the kidnapper to a narrow lane near Oxspring in South Yorkshire. By now conditions were foggy and the radio link was breaking up. Finally, he was stopped by a traffic cone in the middle of the road and a sign telling him to put the money in a wooden tray resting on top of a wall at the roadside, then to move the cone and drive on.

LEFT
Kevin Watts, manager of the estate agency where kidnap victim Stephanie Slater worked, was directed from one public telephone booth to another towards the final rendezvous.

ABOVE
The trail led him as far as a traffic cone with a note ordering him to stop and place the money in a wooden tray alongside the road, before driving on.

The police reached the spot only to find the money gone. The wall was the parapet of a bridge where the road crossed a disused railway track, and they concluded the kidnapper must have tugged a rope attached to the tray to cause the money to fall to where he was waiting with a motor-cycle. He was then able to make his escape along the disused trackbed, and evade the police search. Four hours later a shaken and disoriented Stephanie Slater was dropped outside a house in Great Barr from an orange Metro car which then left the scene at high speed.

Careful questioning of Stephanie filled in a lot more details of the kidnapper. The details of the hunt were released to the press, together with an artist's impression and a recording of his voice from the various telephone calls. He was also identified as the person responsible for kidnapping and killing Julie Dart, which resulted in the police receiving a long and rambling letter claiming he was not the same person, nor was he the same person who had threatened to derail an express train, though he claimed that person had somehow been able to gain access to his word processor to issue his demands. Nevertheless, the net was tightening. Following a revue of the evidence on national television, police received a call from one Susan Oake of Keighley in Yorkshire, who told them the voice was almost certainly that of her ex-husband Michael Sams.

Police checked and found Michael Sams was 51 years old, owned an orange Metro, had previous convictions for deception and fraud, and was a keen railway buff. He had three failed marriages and a series of unsuccessful business ventures had left him short of funds. He admitted to the kidnapping of Stephanie Slater but refused to admit to killing Julie Dart, and at his trial in July 1993, claimed that she had been killed by a friend who had borrowed Sams' typewriter to produce the ransom note. On July 8, he was found guilty by the jury and sentenced to life imprisonment. Four days later he finally admitted to detectives that he had been responsible for Julie's murder.

LEFT
Kevin Watts with the ransom money which was later picked up by the kidnapper, and resulted in the release of Stephanie Slater.

ABOVE
Stephanie Slater after her release, at a police press conference – a television broadcast resulted in a phone call from the ex-wife of Michael Sams, who recognized a tape recording of his voice making ransom demands.

'Irs. Reso,

Recapping the procedure.

1. You should have $18.5 million in used $100 bills
   equally distribuited in 10 Eddie Bauer green colored
   laundry bags.

2. You should be driving your white station wagon.

3. Your daughter and J. 'Iorakis should be with you.

4. Any attempt at surveillance will result in our ending this
   process and the resulting death of your husband.

5. Any interference with the pick up will result in
   the death of your husband and the death of another Exxon
   employee.

6. 'Irs. Reso should answer all telephone calls. She will be
   asked questions that only she can answer.

7. Follow all directions exactly. You will be observed
   at several points during the delivery.

8. Shortly after the delivery you will be contacted with
   instructions including the time and place of your husbands
   release.

and demands for more coded newspaper classified ads attempted to set up another exchange. At last, on June 18, the team carrying the ransom and cell phone, as instructed, in the Reso family's station wagon were given a succession of instructions leading them along a complex route by a series of calls made from local public call boxes, and messages left at specified locations. At last, at 10.40 in the evening, the surveillance team in a shopping mall in the town of Chester spotted a white male using a call box which was identified as the source of a call to the cell phone in the ransom car. They followed the suspect to a rental car and took down the license number as he drove off.

Thirty-six minutes later, a different surveillance team saw a white female using a call box in the town of Gladstone which was traced as the source of another call to the ransom car. After another series of complex directions, the car carrying the ransom was

ABOVE
The ransom note left at a nearby shopping mall and addressed to the victim's wife, setting down the rules she had to follow to secure his release.

directed to the Far Hills railway station. Seven minutes later, at 11.28 a surveillance team saw the hire car carrying the first suspect driving into the station parking lot, stopping and waiting before driving off again. Later the same car was spotted by another surveillance team, but they lost it. The FBI and the local police went to the car hire depot to check out details of the hirers, when much to their surprise both suspects turned up at a quarter to one the following morning to return the car, and were immediately arrested.

The suspects were revealed as Arthur and Jackie Seale. Far from being an environmental activist, Arthur Seale was a former policeman, and later a security officer at Exxon who had targeted Reso as a potential target for extorting a sum of money large enough to pay off his considerable business debts, and provide a new life in the sun for himself and his wife. They had watched their target's movements very carefully and noted that on some occasions he was picked up from home by a company limousine, but on other days he drove to work in his own car. When he was driving, he always stopped at the end of his drive to pick up his copy of the daily newspaper, and all they had to do was move the newspaper to the other side of the drive, so that he would have to stop his car, climb out of the driving seat, and walk round the car to pick up the paper. When he did that, the Seales were waiting in cover at the roadside, and were able to seize him at gunpoint and transport him into captivity in a waiting van.

A week after her arrest, Jackie Seale pleaded guilty to charges of kidnapping and extortion, and took the police to the Bass River State Forest at the southern end of New Jersey, where the body of Sidney Reso had been buried in a shallow grave. Although it had been their intention to keep him alive and release him after the ransom was paid, he had suffered a heart attack after five days confined with little to eat or drink, blindfolded, gagged, and handcuffed in a coffin-like wooden box. An additional factor had been that, during the struggle when he had originally been seized, Reso had been wounded in the arm when Seale's gun went off accidentally. Arthur Seale eventually entered a guilty plea to the charges of murder, kidnapping, and extortion, and was sentenced to life imprisonment, while his wife was given a 20-year sentence for extortion.

BELOW
Arthur Seale outside the court during his trial in which he pleaded guilty to the kidnapping and murder of Sidney Reso, and an extortion attempt on Exxon International.

Rodney Whitchelo

Extortion from the Inside

MANY THREATS TO CONTAMINATE FOOD on store shelves turn out to be clumsy attempts to blackmail the producers or the retailers into handing over money. The first problem for the police is to decide whether a given threat is serious or not, and in this respect a profiler can often provide valuable information from the contents and presentation of the ransom note. In the case of one of the worst poisoning campaigns in Britain, profiler Paul Britton was able to tell from a letter sent to the managing director of Pedigree Petfoods in August 1988 that on this occasion, the blackmailer seemed to know what he was talking about.

Accompanying the letter was a can of dog food which, according to the author of the letter, had been opened, contaminated with colorless, odorless, and highly toxic chemicals and then soldered and resealed to conceal the evidence of the tampering beneath the label. Unless the company handed over a phased ransom of £100,000 each year for five years into specially set-up building society accounts, further contaminated cans would be placed on the shelves of five different supermarkets each day, until sales slumped to vanishing point. After that, another of the company's products would be targeted, and eventually the company would be forced out of business, providing a powerful example to other petfood manufacturers which the blackmailer would then approach.

The tone of the letter, the language used, and even the amount of the ransom suggested an

ABOVE
Jars of Heinz baby food which extortionist Rodney Whitchelo threatened to contaminate with caustic soda, unless the manufacturers paid him a ransom

organized criminal rather than a psychotic individual with a grudge against the company. The evidence of the contaminated can suggested he had the skill to open and reseal the cans himself, and the whole operation suggested someone with the patience and dedication to mount a carefully planned campaign. Britton's profile suggested the blackmailer was of mature years, average or above average in intelligence, educated to secondary school level and probably working on his own.

His plan for collecting the ransom was unusual but effective. As a condition of the threat, accounts had to be opened in specified building societies, and the cash cards and PIN numbers for those accounts had to be mailed to a large number of accommodation addresses, to make police surveillance all but impossible. Once he had picked up the cards, they would allow the blackmailer to withdraw money from the various accounts at thousands of ATM or cash machines all over the country, without the danger of being trapped or identified. As the money was paid, it was clear that he never returned to the same ATM machine, which made surveillance impossible.

When Pedigree Petfoods, on police advice, tried to regain the initiative by delaying some of the payments into the accounts and blaming the society for the problems, the threats became more strident, and as a further demonstration of the blackmailer's powers, warning calls were made to draw attention to cans clearly marked as "contaminated" left at three different supermarkets. When opened, they were found to contain razor blades hidden in the dog food. At last the blackmailer seemed to run out of patience, and demanded the balance of the full £500,000 be paid immediately.

The blackmailer chooses new targets

By this time, a statistical analysis of the pattern of the locations of all the ATM machines where the withdrawals of ransom money had been made suggested the blackmailer lived in the area close to London, with a possible location of Hornchurch in Essex, to the east of the capital. By March 1989, his demands had escalated to £1.25 million and 14 spiked cans had been found, though a warning call had been made in each case. When the threats and demands stopped, it appeared the blackmailer

clever idea for collecting the ransom was in fact based on someone else's extortion attempt, where a blackmailer had threatened to murder millionaire turkey farmer Bernard Matthews, and used a similar method for collecting the cash. In this earlier case though, the blackmailer had continued to make repeated visits to the same small number of cash machines, which lead to his eventual capture and imprisonment. The blackmailer in the Heinz case, however, seemed to know when major surveillance campaigns were being mounted as no withdrawals were made in those areas. It was at least worth considering whether he was a retired police officer, or one currently suspended or on sick leave, possibly with contacts on the investigation team.

In this case, the company's first policy was to refuse to give in to the blackmailer's threats.

> "The tone of the letter, the language used, and even the amount of the ransom suggested an organized criminal rather than a psychotic individual with a grudge against the company." Paul Britton's analysis of the letter sent to Pedigree Petfoods by Rodney Whitchelo

had grown tired of the game. However, on March 22, the Heinz company received a similar letter to the one originally sent to Pedigree. This time, the target had shifted — the police were sent a jar of Heinz baby food that had been contaminated with highly corrosive caustic soda. This was easily obtained from hardware stores as a drain cleaner, and it was easy to mix the colorless compound with the contents of the jar.

By now it was becoming clearer to Paul Britton that the blackmailer knew so much about police investigations and the dangers inherent in collecting his ransom money that it was highly likely he had been a policeman himself. His motivation was likely to involve demonstrating his cleverness at outwitting the authorities, rather than simple greed, which suggested his career had suffered what he would consider to have been an unfair setback. His

One mother suffered caustic soda burns from opening a jar of baby food, and an infant was cut around the mouth from razor blade fragments in a jar of yogurt. For the first time, no warnings had been given, and it seemed likely the blackmailer had been angered by the refusal to negotiate. Furthermore, when details were published in the press to guard against further injuries, a flood of copy-cat claims seeking to benefit from the main campaign.

Heinz were forced to undertake the same arrangements as Pedigree Petfoods had been, paying money into building society accounts from which the blackmailer could withdraw cash from different ATM machines. In the meantime, Heinz withdrew products from stores where contaminated containers had been found, and they spent millions developing new, tamper-proof packaging that would reveal if the containers had been opened after manufacture.

The police tried monitoring all the different accommodation addresses where the cash cards and PIN numbers had been sent, but the blackmailer seemed to know what was going on, and stayed clear. Finally, a letter containing some strange misspellings, like "syanide" for "cyanide" to suggest a semi-literate author, was sent to the police asking for a reward of £50,000 for naming the blackmailer, and even mentioning the secret code-name for the surveillance operation. Though the writer had tried to suggest this was a completely different person from the blackmailer, close inspection by the police revealed it was almost certainly written by their adversary, and they had to accept there was a leak from within the team.

A new team was formed, working under the greatest secrecy, and while trying to discern a pattern in the cash withdrawals, they decided to target ATM machines belonging to the Woolwich Building Society in the London area. At last, in the early hours of the morning of October 21, 1989, officers watching a machine in Enfield, on the northern edge of London, saw a bearded man park a car nearby and walk over to the machine, carrying a crash helmet with him. When they stopped him, they recognized him, and he fainted. He was Rodney Whitchelo, a former detective from the London Regional Crime Squad, who lived in Hornchurch and who had actually been a member of the investigation team brought in when the focus of the blackmail campaign had shifted from Pedigree to Heinz.

He had previously worked on the ransom case on which his own was based where the building society cash machine ransom arrangements had been used, and the man responsible jailed, and had still been working as a detective sergeant when he sent the original letter to Pedigree. Several months later, he had resigned on the grounds of ill health, which gave him the extra time he needed to visit cash machines over a wide area of the country, but he continued to socialize with members of the investigation teams and was told about plans and progress of the hunt for the blackmailer. On one occasion he had even been sitting in the back of a car manned by former colleagues who were watching to see if the blackmailer called at a particular accommodation address!

Finally, late in 1990, Rodney Whitchelo was found guilty of six charges of blackmail and was sentenced to 17 years in prison. As a direct consequence of his extortion campaign, the entire food industry had to change its packaging to provide positive evidence to the purchaser if a can, jar, or package had been opened after manufacture — for example, once a jar is opened, a vacuum seal is broken allowing a button on the lid to be pressed in. If that button can be pressed on a jar taken from the shelf, the customer is warned to reject it.

LEFT
Rodney Whitchelo seemed to know so much about the police hunt for him that profiler Paul Britton concluded correctly that he must have had police connections.

CHAPTER NINE

SIGNATURE
CRIME ANALYSIS

9: Signature crime analysis

Howomever carefully a criminal may plan and carry out a crime, the crime scene will supply police and criminal analysts with a wealth of different kinds of information as to how and why, and by whom, that particular crime was committed. Much of this information can reveal what kind of person committed the crime, making it possible to narrow down the search to a particular type of suspect. Some will be classic forensic evidence that can help to confirm — once a particular suspect has been identified and arrested — whether or not that individual actually committed that particular crime.

Some information will relate to the identity of the individual, like blood samples and fingerprints. Some will relate to how the crime was actually committed — to the modus operandi, or MO of the criminal. However, in some cases information will reveal a much more secret and more individual picture of the offender involved. Some crime scene details will reveal the specific emotional needs and drives of the perpetrator, which resulted in him committing the crime in the first place. This is often referred to as the "signature" of the criminal.

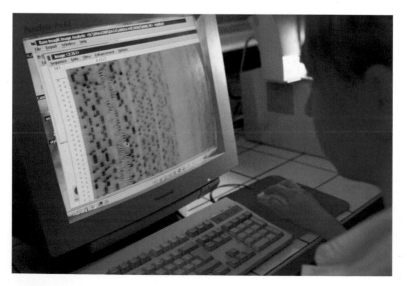

The distinction between MO evidence and signature evidence is often blurred. For example, a particular criminal may use a gun to threaten his victims and force them to do what he wants. This is normally part of the MO. He uses the gun to impose his will on the victim, since he might lack the physical strength needed to force someone else to obey his demands. Using the gun is an essential part of what is making it possible for him to commit the crime. In the simplest terms, it relates to HOW the crime was committed.

Signature evidence, on the other hand, relates to WHY the crime was committed. In cases where the criminal subjects his victims to torture while he has them in his power, this almost certainly represents a "signature" aspect of the crime. There is no need for him to torture his victims, simply to make it possible for him to commit the crime. The torture is inflicted purely to satisfy the criminal's own sadistic needs, and is one of the reasons he chose to commit the crime in the first place.

MO — or signature?

The distinction between MO and signature evidence becomes most important when examining a series of crimes possibly committed by the same offender. Frequently, the MO may change as the offender becomes more confident and more experienced. As a burglar becomes more efficient at breaking into houses, he may change his methods to avoid previous errors and mistakes. If he smashes a window, the risk of the noise being overheard means he has only a limited time to search the house in case witnesses come to investigate. Once he learns how to force locks quietly, he not only suffers less danger

LEFT
Crime officer dusting a broken window for fingerprints, using magnesium powder, while investigating a break-in and robbery.

of capture but has more time to search for valuables and make his visit more profitable.

In all aspects involving the MO, the offender normally shows no reluctance to make these improvements. In the case of a career criminal, being caught and sent to prison will almost certainly result in improvements to his MO, should he continue offending after release. Time in prison provides plenty of opportunity to review every detail of his crimes, and isolate the mistakes which led to his being arrested. In addition, the chance to discuss them with other more experienced prisoners is almost bound to result in changes to make his routine MO more effective.

In the case of crimes against individuals, the victim's response to the criminal also produces changes in the MO. When a rape victim fights back against his attack, to the point where the offender has problems in controlling the victim, he will usually respond by changing the MO. Instead of relying on weapons like knives or blunt instruments he might find at the scene of the crime, or using materials found on the spot to restrain his victim, he tends to bring these necessities with him instead, like duct tape to bind the victim and subdue her resistance.

He may also increase the violence of his initial assault, so that the victim becomes incapacitated from the start. In extreme cases, the criminal may finally kill the victim if all his attempts to crush her resistance prove ineffective. But these are all acts

ABOVE
Yorkshire, England –
detectives investigate the
body of yet another victim of
serial killer Peter Sutcliffe,
the Yorkshire Ripper.

intended to make it possible for him to carry out the rape, rather than objectives in their own right. As they relate to how the crime was carried out rather than why, they remain part of a developing MO rather than a signature.

Signature evidence obeys a completely different set of rules. Because these aspects are much more personal to the individual criminal, they tend to be much less flexible. He is much less able to change, or even want to change, these parts of his routine. If he enjoys torturing and inflicting fear and pain on his victims, he will continue torturing future victims, since he would otherwise have no reason to carry out the crimes at all.

The only changes which may happen in his signature are evolutionary ones, from a heightening need for emotional release. A torturer may intensify the pain and suffering he inflicts on successive victims as a way to maintain the satisfaction he derives from his crimes as his experience grows. Nevertheless, the overall theme will remain the same throughout, as this is linked to his main reasons for committing the crimes.

In the same way, a murderer who mutilates his victims after killing them, like Jack the Ripper, may inflict more savage mutilations with succeeding attacks. These too will be differences of degree rather than changes in the basic signature. Because of this resistance to change, signature elements are particularly important in analyzing an individual crime, since they can suggest a link between these and other cases where a similar signature was found. However, there are cases where signatures may show missing elements on specific occasions because of unexpected events. These can include meeting a different response from a victim or being interrupted while carrying out the ritual of the crime.

Deciphering the signature

Identifying signature elements means separating them from those relating to the MO. FBI profiler John Douglas in a paper on MO, signature, and staging, uses a fictitious example to explain the basic difference between MO and signature. A rapist enters a house to find his intended victim and her partner. To commit the crime, he has to prevent the partner from attacking him or raising the alarm. If he restrains him by tying him up or locking him in another room, he achieves his objective. But if instead he ties the

BELOW
Terrorist bombers operate from different motives – this is the Bali bombing of a night club in October 2002 – but can still show signature aspects in their weapons and the carrying out of the crime.

man up and then forces him to witness his partner being raped, this becomes part of a pattern of inflicting pain, humiliation, and domination on both his victims, and is likely to be an important part of his signature. As such, it may well be repeated whenever he attacks women with partners on the premises.

Another example devised by John Douglas was that of a bank robber with an ingenious way of delaying the bank staff from calling the police after his escape. He forces them to strip, predicting that only when they find their clothes and get dressed will they actually call for help. This would be a good example of an ingenious MO, designed purely to make committing the crime more efficient and arrest less likely. Only if the robber had then used the temporary power he had over the bank staff to force them to strip, and then compelled them to allow him to photograph them in suggestive and degrading poses, does his objective shift from committing the basic crime to satisfying his own emotional needs, crossing the boundary between MO and signature.

ABOVE
The terrible aftermath of a terrorist bomb: a victim of the Istanbul bombing of November 2003 prays in the wreckage of the Neve Shalom synagogue.

Even bombers and arsonists can show signatures. The way a fire is started is part of the arsonist's MO, since this makes it possible for him to burn down a building. In some cases, the blaze may not be the primary objective. It may be intended to cover up evidence of a different crime — to suggest a murder victim died in an accidental fire for example. This too, would be part of the MO since it relates to a rational reason for committing the crime.

Signature on the other hand relates to why the arsonist sets light to a building, where no logical reason seems to exist. The kind of building targeted may be part of the criminal's signature. Other evidence of any personal rituals carried out by the criminal on the premises before the fire took hold would also be part of the signature. Some carry out acts of vandalism, others may urinate or defecate at the scene. None of these acts play a part in burning down the building, but are essential to the offender's psychological needs and therefore form part of his signature.

Bombers act from a variety of motives. They may have a political objective, or a score to settle, or want to destroy property. Equally, they may derive satisfaction from spreading terror or inflicting death or injury on as many victims as possible. The technicalities of the weapon like the type of explosive, the casing, the trigger, and the detonator normally form parts of the

MO, as essential features of the method of committing the crime. Signature factors emerge when the bomber makes changes to the bomb to intensify the destruction or injury. He might add nails to a pipe bomb to create shrapnel, or strengthen the structure of the bomb to hold it together for a fractionally longer time after detonation, and greatly intensify the blast. All suggest the level of anger or hatred felt by the perpetrator towards those intended to be on the receiving end of his weapon, whether innocent and random passers-by or specific targets for his revenge.

Why signature matters

Because signature aspects of successive crimes committed by the same criminal tend to be consistent compared with MOs, they give criminal analysts an important means for linking crimes to a common perpetrator. Where it is perfectly possible for different crimes in a particular area at a particular time to show similar MOs, these may be committed by different people. In cases where signatures remain unchanged though, there is a strong probability these crimes may well have been committed by the same offender.

There are two reasons why this kind of analysis is vital. Individual murders are terrible crimes, but are usually related to a particular set of motives — a grudge, a vendetta, a breakdown of a relationship, or a need to silence a witness or an opponent —

which are relatively unlikely to recur. In the case of a serial killer or rapist, though, the drives to commit the crime are provided by his own psychological make-up, and often cause violent attacks at much closer intervals, unless he is identified and caught. This means that identifying a series of rapes or murders as the work of an individual serial offender imposes an even greater priority on the need to identify and catch the person responsible.

The other reason relates to the negative information given by signature analysis. Sometimes this can show that an individual almost certainly did not commit a given crime. The classic case of David Vasquez, cited by John

BELOW
Careful profiling work secured the release of David Vasquez when another crime with a closely similar signature to the one for which he was convicted was carried out while he was serving his sentence.

Douglas, is an example of how recognizing the signature aspects of two different murders helped to free an innocent man who had been jailed for the first of the killings.

Vasquez entered a plea of guilty in 1984 to the murder of a 34-year-old woman in Arlington, Virginia. The victim had been strangled with a ligature, and left lying face down, with her hands tied behind her back, and she had been sexually assaulted. Signature aspects included elaborate bindings with highly unusual knots, and a lead connecting the victim's wrists to her neck over her left shoulder. In addition, the body was left openly on display, to present the maximum shock value to anyone who discovered the victim.

Crime scene analysis showed the killer had spent a relatively long time with the victim. The elaborate bindings had taken time to prepare, but allowed a high degree of control over the victim. He had moved her from one room to another around the house, and had at one time taken her into the bathroom and made her clean her teeth. This behavior was not necessary to make it possible to commit the attack and murder, so it related to the killer's own needs and signature rather than his MO.

If Vasquez was not the killer, why did he confess? He had a lower than normal IQ, and his lawyers believed they would find it difficult to prove his innocence. They convinced him that by pleading innocent and then being found guilty, he risked the death penalty. If he entered a plea of guilty, he would almost certainly be given life imprisonment.

Vasquez had served three years of his life sentence when in 1987 police found another murder victim. The body of a 44-year-old woman was found lying face down with her hands tied behind her back. Once again, the rope had been fastened with unusual and elaborate knots, with a strand leading from her neck to her wrists. Once again, she had been strangled with a ligature and sexually assaulted. Once again, the killer spent a relatively long time at the scene, and left her body exposed. It was just four blocks away from the first murder in 1984.

The local police department asked the National Center for the Analysis of Violent Crime (NCAVC) to carry out a detailed analysis of these two murders, together with a series of sexual assaults and several other killings that occurred in the area during that same three-year period. Eventually, the NCAVC report was able to link these cases through signature similarities to that of a local suspect. This conclusion was later supported by physical evidence, and ruled out the possibility that David Vasquez had indeed carried out the first killing. He was released from prison and officially cleared of the crime.

Types of signature evidence

Signature evidence can be as varied as the motives and fantasies of the criminals. In cases involving rape and murder, the manner in which the victim was killed may involve both the MO and the signature of the criminal. Items left at the crime scene, or trophies taken from the victim, like locks of hair or articles of clothing, can also be part of the signature, as can the position in which the victim's body has been left. Where the victim survives, the attitude and behavior of the criminal and the words he used during the attack are also valuable signature evidence. And where the victim's body is found at the scene, visible wounds or marks in the form of post-mortem mutilation normally relate to the signature rather than the MO.

In killings where the attacker carries a firearm, the victims would normally be shot, unless the danger of someone hearing the noise of the shots was a major factor. But in cases like the Code killings (*see* pages 91-93) the killer went far beyond the degree of violence needed to subdue and kill those he attacked, slashing their throats and in one instance almost beheading the victim, showing clear evidence of his signature. That extra degree of violence is one reason why he committed the murders in the first place.

FBI profiler Roy Hazelwood, working with psychiatrist Dr Park Dietz in studying a group of 30 male sexually sadistic criminals found they were relatively willing to talk about the details of the violent acts they had committed, as these were more related to the MO for their crimes. However, they were much more reluctant to talk about their sexual acts or fantasies, since these were much more personal matters, and were therefore closely related to the signature aspects of their crimes.

BELOW
A gun is carefully removed from a crime scene. Killers who use firearms run the risk of the shots being heard. When a gun has been used, the gunshot wounds tend to be the last wounds a victim receives because shooting is less personal than stabbing or strangling.

George Russell

The Yuppie Killer

LIKE MANY ANGER-DRIVEN SERIAL KILLERS, George Russell wanted his victims dead as quickly as possible, to allow him to exert complete control over their lifeless bodies, in a ritual that he developed further with each succeeding murder. The background to his crimes was the upmarket community of Bellevue in the state of Washington in the Pacific Northwest of the U.S. Though Russell himself was black, and something of a drifter and petty criminal, he had been brought up in an affluent upper middle-class family, and he had the appearance and confidence to fit into the local social life of this predominantly white area, especially its thriving singles bars and restaurants.

His first victim was 27-year-old Mary Ann Pohlreich, whose body was found in an alleyway between a branch of McDonald's and a restaurant called The Black Angus, in the early morning of June 23, 1990. It was clear that her naked body had been deliberately posed by her killer. She was lying on her back in plain view in an area where she was bound to be seen. Her left foot was crossed over her right ankle, and her arms were bent across her stomach with her hands touching, and grasping a large fir cone. Her head was turned to the left with a plastic food container placed carefully over her right eye.

No items of her clothing were found at the scene, though she was still wearing a neck chain and a wristwatch. Witness statements and the post mortem revealed she had probably been killed elsewhere and brought to the alley deliberately. She had been strangled and subjected to several massive blows, and post-mortem abrasions to her body showed she had been dragged to her present location, possibly from an original location further back in a nearby pile of rubbish. She had been vaginally raped and her anal area was damaged by a foreign object which was not found at the scene.

She had last been seen around ten o'clock the previous evening, leaving a singles bar called Papagayo's Cantina, about a mile away from where her body was found, and her car was still in the car park. It seemed she had left with a date, and had not been seen alive again.

The next victim was found on August 9 in a very different location. Carol Beethe, a single mother of two young daughters, was discovered in bed at her Bellevue home, some two miles away from the location of the first victim's body. She worked behind the bar of another singles haunt called the Cucina Cucina restaurant, and had last been seen at 2.30 that morning entering her house alone. Her body was found on her bed, naked except for a pair of red high-heeled shoes on her feet, with her legs splayed and her own shotgun inserted deep into her vagina. The body was arranged to face the door so that no-one entering the room could avoid the horror of the scene, but her head was covered after death by a plastic bag and then by a pillow, placed so as to suggest suffocation. The post-mortem revealed she had been savagely beaten, with many more blows than would be needed to kill her, with a weapon which left strange, Y-shaped impressions in the skin.

Finally on September 3, 1990, 24-year-old Randi Levine was found in her apartment in the suburb of Kirkland, Washington, some seven miles to the north of the location of the first victim's body. She had been seen leaving a local restaurant called the Maple Gardens alone around midnight four days previously having had a meal with friends, and her body was discovered by the landlord of her apartment block. Her naked body was lying on its back on top of her bed, and she had suffered massive blows to the head, in an attack which almost certainly began while she was still asleep. Her head was covered with a pillow, and a sheet partly covered the upper half of her body. Her

Police ask for clues in slaying

Victim in parking lot identified as Redmond woman

By Patricia Moir
Journal American Staff Writer

A woman found beaten to death Saturday behind a Bellevue restaurant has been identified as Mary Ann Pohlreich, a 27-year-old Redmond resident and former Bellevue Community College student.

Her nude body was found about 7:30 a.m. near a garbage dumpster in

the parking lot at the Black Angus restaurant, 1411 156th Ave. N.E. She died between 2:30 a.m. and 5:30 a.m. from a blow to the head, according to the King County medical examiner's office.

Police learned Pohlreich's identity Tuesday when her roommate, Teresa Veary, returned from a weekend trip and reported her missing. Veary said

Wednesday she knew something was wrong when she found Pohlreich's car in the parking lot of Papagayo's Cantina — a nightspot in the Overlake area where she said Pohlreich went dancing by herself Friday night.

Police want to talk to anyone who saw Pohlreich at Papagayo's, 2239 148th Ave. N.E., or saw her leave

with someone, said Bellevue police spokesman Steve Bourgette.

A bartender working there Friday night did not recognize a picture of Pohlreich provided by police Wednesday.

"We get 600 to 700 people through here on a Friday night," he said.

See **Slaying victim** *on* A10

MARY ANN POHLREICH

ABOVE
Newspaper coverage from the *Journal American*, when Mary Ann Pohlreich, the first of Russell's victims is discovered.

legs were spreadeagled, and a vibrator was placed in her mouth, while a copy of a book titled The Joy of Sex was carefully placed in the crook of her arm. More than 200 cuts had been inflicted all over her body after death, including on the soles of her feet.

In the conventional way of assessing crimes, based on the killer's MO, there was every chance these crimes would have been classified as being the work of at least two killers, because of the discrepancies in the ways in which the crimes were committed. For example, the first victim was attacked while on her way home, and was left in a highly public location, whereas both the second and third victims were killed in their own homes. The first victim was raped, but the others were not, and the types and patterns of wounds were different in each case.

However, looked at from the viewpoint of the killer's signature, these crimes followed a much more consistent pattern. Chief criminal investigator Bob Keppel decided that from the first, the killer was building a progressively more demanding and detailed fantasy which showed an escalating pattern over all three murders. Mary Anne Pohlreich showed a variety of defence wounds, which indicated that the killer had a relatively difficult job subduing and killing her. Nevertheless, he had felt confident enough to take her to such a public place and leave her body, undressed and carefully posed, to make sure it fitted his own personal agenda.

In the case of Carol Beethe, he was able to kill her in a location which seemed much more secure, although her young daughters were asleep in the house at the time. This suggested

he attacked her while she was asleep and therefore unable to raise the alarm. The post mortem showed far fewer defence wounds, indicating she had been killed more quickly than the first victim, leaving the killer with even more time to display her according to his fantasy, but the level of violence meted out to the body of the victim was escalating appreciably from that perpetrated on that of the first victim.

Finally, Randi Levine represented the apex of the progression so far. Once again, she had been attacked while asleep, and the killer was spending an even longer time with the body, inflicting such an apparently endless succession of wounds on the lifeless corpse. The details of the posing of the body after death followed the pattern established in the first two killings, and the killer was clearly growing more confident and more demanding in the ritual he followed in each case.

The Bellevue Yuppie Murders, as they became known, involved the work of profilers, though not in this case to identify the killer. The requirement here was to ensure that the principal suspect was convicted of all three murders, as the evidence linking suspect to victim was stronger in one case than in the other two. On the other hand, if the court accepted that the signature evidence showed a strong probability that all three women were killed by the same man, then the overall case was greatly strengthened as a result.

In spite of his middle-class background, George Russell already had a criminal record as a trespasser and a possessor of stolen property. When he was a young boy, his parents had split up when his mother left home, leaving George to be raised by his father. Later she had returned for him, together with another man, and eventually abandoned that relationship too, leaving George to fend for himself as a young man, and nurture feelings of resentment toward a mother he felt had repeatedly let him down.

He was first linked to the murders when a local detective arrested him after a brawl, for impersonating a police officer and carrying a concealed firearm. The serial number on the gun revealed it had been stolen from a property in the same area as that of the third victim's home. The breakthrough came on September 12, nine days after Randi Levine's body was discovered. A woman called to complain of a prowler in Bellevue, and police turned up to find George Russell walking away from the area. Russell was arrested and DNA samples were taken and compared with that found on the first victim. The evidence showed he was Mary Ann Pohlreich's killer. Police traced the friend's pick-up he had used to transport the body and found traces of the victim's blood in the vehicle.

But had he carried out the other two murders? FBI profiler John Douglas was asked to analyze the crimes and he found a series of links between the three killings. First of all, he considered the blitz-type attacks which were part of the killer's MO were highly consistent, which was likely to be the case in killings which were only weeks apart. But he was convinced the signature aspects of the crimes were even more significant. Although it was unusual to find a black serial killer attacking white women, Russell had grown up in a predominantly white community and was confident in these surroundings. One of the most significant links in the signature had been the placing of victims where, in spite of the differences between the locations, they were certain to be found relatively quickly. The bodies were left exposed, and were deliberately arranged in as degrading a pose as possible, spread out as if for sex with additional props like the fir-cone, the shotgun, and the vibrator arranged to reinforce the message. As a result of the signature evidence, the authorities agreed to try the three murders together, and George Russell was found guilty of all three and sentenced to life imprisonment.

BELOW
An article taken from the *Journal American*, Bellevue, at the time of Russell's trial.

Russell's defense: It's not me

By Christopher Jarvis
Journal American Staff Writer

The wrong man sits at a defense table in King County Superior Court accused of three of the most "outrageous" murders in state history, a jury heard Thursday.

In opening statements, defense attorneys started their assault on the state's case against former Mercer Island resident George W. Russell, accused of the slayings last summer of three young Eastside women.

Russell, clad in a Navy blue sports coat, gray slacks, a white shirt and tie, sat intently as attorneys outlined the evidence jurors will hear in his trial on one count of first-degree murder and two counts of aggravated first-degree murder.

The 33-year-old Russell periodically took notes as jurors heard how evidence will show he either did or did not kill Mary Ann Pohlreich, 27, Carol Marie Beethe, 35, and Andrea S. "Randi" Levine, 24, in a 67-day span from June 23, 1990 to Aug. 31, 1990.

"The evidence will show the wrong person is sitting here on trial and we will be asking for a verdict of not guilty," defense attorney Miriam Schwartz said.

Schwartz systematically attacked state evidence in the case saying that scientific evidence linking Russell to Pohlreich's killing is unreliable and unable to positively link him to her rape and killing.

Pohlreich's body was found lying next to a garbage dumpster posed in a fashion prosecutors say is "inconsistent" with the violent nature of her death.

Schwartz said some of the evidence — semen found during an autopsy — implicates not only Russell, but also 8 percent of the population, which amounts to as many as 200,000 residents of the Puget Sound region.

"I ask you to rely on reliable evidence" in considering the case against Russell, Schwartz said.

In the death of Beethe, whose beaten, nude body was found in the bedroom of her east Bellevue home on Aug. 9, 1990, Schwartz suggested that her boyfriend had both opportunity and motive for the killing. Beethe and the man had a falling out earlier in the summer and she was seeing another man, Schwartz said.

See **Russell** on A12

George W. Russell, on trial for the slayings of three Eastside women, consults with his lawyers prior to rejecting a plea bargain.

Jeffrey Dahmer

Killer and Cannibal

PERPHAPS THE MOST NOTORIOUS serial killer of all time, Jeffrey Dahmer, also had the clearest and most bizarre signatures of all, in contrast to a range of different MOs he used to trap, kill, and keep his victims. Dahmer's career as a killer began in 1978, in Richfield, Ohio, when was eighteen years old and had recently graduated from high school. He picked up a young man, 19-year-old hitch-hiker Steven Mark Hicks, and took him back to his home where he was living alone while his parents were away. There the two drank beer and had sex. When Hicks got up to leave, Dahmer became anxious at the thought of being left on his own and tried to force Hicks to stay. When he insisted on leaving Dahmer picked up a bar-bell and hit Hicks a very hard blow to the head, resulting in his death. Dahmer then buried the body outside, but after a couple of weeks he dug it up, dismembered it, took the flesh off the bones, dissolved it in acid and flushed it into the drains. The bones he smashed into small fragments which he scattered in the woodland surrounding the house.

This was the start of a killing career that lasted for 13 years. He picked up young men, had sex with them and killed them in a variety of ways before using their lifeless remains in progressively more bizarre rituals. Though he managed to find and kill victims while living in his grandmother's house or staying in hotel rooms, his fantasies became much more intense when he set up home in his own apartment in

"Yes, I do have remorse, but I'm not even sure myself whether it is as profound as it should be. I've always wondered myself why I don't feel more remorse." Jeffrey Dahmer

RIGHT

RIGHT
Police removing an acid tank from Dahmer's apartment – the acid was used to dissolve the bodies of his victims and for injecting into the brains of his live captives to turn them into compliant zombies.

OPPOSITE
Jeffrey Dahmer listens to the charges against him at the Milwaukee County Circuit Court on the July 25, 1991 of four counts of first-degree intentional homicide.

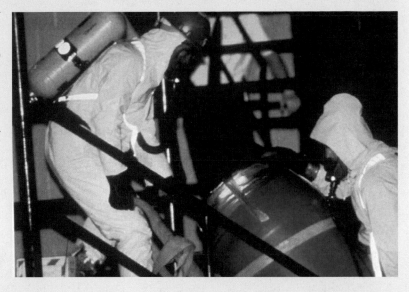

"I took the knife and the scalp part off and peeled the flesh off the bone and kept the skull and the scalp... If I could have kept him longer, all of him, I would have."

Jeffrey Dahmer about Anthony Sears

Milwaukee in 1988. This he protected with security locks and bolts, and equipped with freezers to store bodies and body parts and a vat for dissolving human remains in acid.

With this secure base he embarked on a long and successful career, preying on young gay men. He would pick his victims from the streets and shopping malls, and from the gay bars of Milwaukee, or meet them at events like the gay pride march in Chicago. In all cases, he took care to be seen as little as possible with each new victim, and to choose people as far as possible who followed a transient lifestyle, so that they would not be missed too quickly. He would then lure them to his apartment by offering them money to pose for Polaroids.

His routine usually followed the same set pattern. He brought the men he picked up back to his apartment, drugged them then killed them, usually by strangulation. Sometimes he would have sex with them before the killing, but his usual pleasure was to have sex with the lifeless corpse after death. Faced with a partner who could not reject him by leaving, Dahmer then derived more and more pleasure from extending his control over the corpse, dismembering it and often eating parts of it, before wearing skin and muscle tissue as bizarre garments, and displaying the heads of his victims as trophies to decorate his apartment. To give him the maximum time for these activities, he would try wherever possible to find and kill a victim on a Friday, leaving the weekend free for his progressively more bizarre experimentation.

Dahmer covered his tracks so well that he was never made the subject of a profile, since most of his victims were simply filed as missing without trace, and no-one suspected Milwaukee was blighted by a deadly serial killer. He had some astonishingly narrow escapes during his career. When driving to the local refuse dump to dispose of the body of his first victim, Steven Hicks, the beer he had drunk caused him to veer erratically across the road, and the police pulled him up. He managed to talk his way out of a possible arrest and search of his car, but was so shaken that he took Hicks' body back to his home and buried it there.

His luck continued. Later, he decided to experiment with ways of prolonging the lives of his victims while turning them into compliant automatons who would remain with him and be entirely subordinate to his control. He would drug his victims and while they were unconscious, drill holes into their skulls so he could inject acid into the frontal lobes of their brains. One died under the treatment, and two more simply complained of headaches when they woke up, so he went on to kill them anyway — their complaints made it clear they were not under his control. But another, a 14-year-old boy named Konerak Sinthasomphone, managed to escape from the apartment and attract the attention of neighbors. They called the police, who could make no sense of what the by now severely confused boy was trying to tell them, so when Dahmer claimed to be a friend, the police released the victim back into

the killer's clutches, after which he gave his victim an additional injection into the brain that killed him.

The end of Dahmer's thirteen years of killing came on the evening of July 23, 1991, when a Milwaukee police car was flagged down by a partially clad young black man who had a set of handcuffs dangling from one wrist. His name was Tracy Edwards and he told the two officers he had been attacked and gave them an address in 924 North 25th Street, Oxford Apartments. When they knocked on the door of apartment 213, it was answered by a man who gave the name of Jeffrey Dahmer. They checked his records, which showed he was on probation for an earlier sexual assault and as he had been drinking, he was technically violating the conditions of his parole. This allowed the officers to arrest him and search his apartment. What they saw there horrified them to the core.

"...I was completely swept along with my own compulsion. I don't know how else to put it. It didn't satisfy me completely so maybe I was thinking another one will. Maybe this one will. Maybe this one will, and the numbers start growing and growing and just got out of control, as you can see..." Jeffrey Dahmer

Police mugshot of Jeffrey Dahmer – an angry and sadistic killer who so wanted to control his victims he kept parts of their bodies with him for as long as possible after he murdered them.

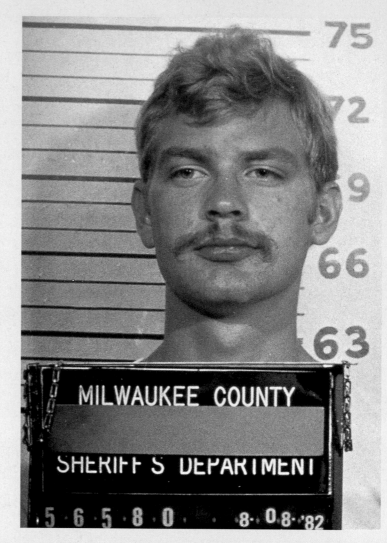

The apartment reeked of rotting meat, and Polaroid prints were scattered around, showing shackled victims alive and dead, and body parts arranged in ritual displays. One showed a victim's skull painted gold, placed carefully on top of his two severed hands palm upwards. Another skull was decomposing in the refrigerator, while more body parts were contained in a large 55-gallon drum in the bedroom of the apartment.

To the experts who analyzed Dahmer and his horrifying rituals, the signature was plain to see. Here was a killer with a lifelong fury and hatred for his victims that seemed to center on his refusal to allow them to leave him after he had lured them to his apartment. The only way for him to have what he wanted from his victims was to keep control and possess them as completely as possible. Therefore, his routine escalated from simply killing, dismembering, and disposing of their remains to feeding on them, wearing parts of their bodies as trophies, and displaying skulls, hands, and sexual organs in his apartment as a way of continuing the possession of his victims. Finally he had tried and failed to extend the possession of those under his control to turn them into automatons to do his absolute bidding while still alive.

The final irony, however, was that he became a victim himself. After starting a life sentence in a high-security prison in the neighboring state of Wisconsin for the killing of 17 young men, he was himself murdered by a fellow inmate on November 28, 1994 at the age of 34.

10: Finding the truth

PROFILING AND CRIME ANALYSIS have proved useful in several respects. They can help narrow down the search for a violent criminal, and can also provide a portrait to be checked against potential suspects. They can also help to show a link between different crimes by exposing a pattern which can identify them as the work of a single criminal. But they have another major benefit, which can be brought into use when a suspect has been identified and arrested, even if factors other than the original analysis led to the final arrest. It can still offer investigating officers a psychological road map to use when questioning their suspect. Because the profile reveals how the criminal thinks and feels about the crime, it can help the interrogators questioning him to navigate their way towards the underlying truth.

How does this work in an individual case? Ronald and Stephen Holmes in *Profiling Violent Crimes — An Investigative Tool* cite the case of a double murder in a small town in the Midwest of the U.S. involving a young couple who were shot. The female victim was 15-year-old Diane Harris and her body was found, together with that of her boyfriend, in her boyfriend's car. Each had been killed by a single shot, Diane by a shot through the temple and her boyfriend by a bullet that entered his body below his left armpit.

There was no physical evidence to reveal who had carried out the murders, but one of the detectives was suspicious of Diane's stepfather. Mr. Harris was an extremely macho football coach of whom many local people were afraid, and under questioning he made an ambiguous remark which could have been a partial admission of guilt. One of the officers had asked him directly if he had killed the two young victims. Harris replied that he had not done so in his "right mind" and the police would have to prove it. When the questioning resumed after a coffee break, he denied the implications of his previous statement, and the investigators made no further progress at all.

After considering Harris's profile as a person with a supreme belief in his own intelligence and masculinity and with a deep need for control, investigators were advised to switch to a different questioning technique. He was taken to a different room in the police headquarters, that had pictures of the crime scene displayed on all four walls. There, the police spoke to their suspect in his role as the recently bereaved stepfather rather than as a potential suspect and admitted they really wanted to solve the murder of his step-daughter but that they were getting nowhere. They needed help, if they were going to be able to explain her death. This approach was calculated to put Harris where he would feel more comfortable, effectively in control of the outcome of the investigation, and he was able to give police pointers on how they should go about looking for the person responsible.

The more he took an active part in discussing the investigation, and the more he talked with police officers about the details of the case, the more engrossed he became in what had happened to his step-daughter and the more subtly the pressure upon him began to build up. Finally, after eight hours of detailed conversation reviewing the crime in the smallest detail, he suddenly broke down in tears. The interrogation was finally resumed after a short pause for him to compose himself, and when the questions began again he surprised his interrogators by freely admitting to the double murder.

The rape of Mary Frances Stoner

For FBI profiler John Douglas, the case which first demonstrated the value of profiling in giving investigators a strategy for questioning their subjects was a crime involving a 12-year-old girl. In this case, it was the horrific rape and murder of Mary Frances Stoner, from the small town of Adairsville in Georgia in

LEFT
The manner in which a suspect is questioned can have a dramatic effect on the behavior of the suspect. As with the the murder of Diane Harris (see above), the officers' apparent alliance with her father actually brought about his confession of guilt.

December 1979. She had been abducted at the end of the driveway to her house, after being dropped by her school bus at the end of the afternoon. Her body was found some days later in a secluded woodland lane some ten miles away.

She had been raped and strangled, but the post mortem revealed the actual cause of her death had been a series of blows to the head, and the murder weapon — a bloodstained rock — was found lying next to the body. Her body was fully dressed. However, the clothes showed signs of being put on in a hurry, one of her shoes was unfastened, and her head was covered by her coat.

Douglas profiled the killer as being a white male in his twenties, who was probably married but with problems which may well have led to a divorce. He would be of average or above average intelligence and educated to high school level, and would have a blue-collar job and a confident, aggressive personality. He may well have done military service, and if so would probably have been discharged for some misdemeanor. He would drive a dark blue or black car and would live locally, and might well already have a criminal record.

The profile assumed local knowledge from the fact that the place where the girl's body had been left would not be known to visitors to the area. The crime showed signs of being a target of opportunity, which meant the criminal had been passing as the girl left the bus, and he reacted instantly to the chance of abducting her. From evidence given by people who knew the victim, she was likely to have been terrified by any threats he had made and would have co-operated up to a point.

The evidence of her clothes suggested she had been made to undress before being raped, and then allowed to put her clothes on again afterwards. Injuries from the rape suggested she must have been in great pain and distress, and at this point it was likely the attacker was finding the situation was passing out of his control. As a local man, she could easily identify him, and it was essential to eliminate the possibility. He must have allowed her to put her clothes back on, but while she was doing so, he had tried to strangle her from behind, possibly to a point where she lost consciousness. To make sure she was dead, he then picked up the nearest weapon to hand — the rock he used to break her skull with two or three massive blows.

BELOW
Coverage from a local newspaper, the *Rome News-Tribune*, reporting on the murder on the day of Mary Frances Stoner's funeral.

Funeral services today *Rome–Cremer–Devier case*

Search continues for clues in brutal weekend slaying

ADAIRSVILLE — Authorities are continuing to search for clues in the slaying of a 12-year-old girl whose body was found Saturday after she was apparently abducted Friday.

Mary Francis Stoner was killed by "a severe blow to the head with a large rock," Bartow County Coroner W.G. Bedford said Sunday. He declined to say if the girl had been sexually molested.

The Bartow County Sheriff's Department said it is looking for a white man, possibly with a beard, who was last seen driving a dark blue compact car. Authorities said a witness reported seeing a person with that description leaving the driveway of the girl's home.

The girl's body was found Saturday in a rural area near her home after a telephone call from "a private citizen who told us he had found the body," said Sgt. Barry Spradley of the sheriff's department.

Miss Stoner, a junior high school majorette and honor student, was apparently abducted about 4 p.m. Friday after stepping off a school bus near her home.

"We have questioned a number of people but we're not holding anybody," investigator Jimmy Spradley said Sunday.

"The FBI, Georgia Bureau of Investigation and other reinforcements

MARY FRANCES STONER

this investigation," said Bedford.

Spradley said that two men had been questioned and released concerning the slaying.

The brutal incident has left the residents of this usually sleepy Northwest Georgia town reeling in shock.

Funeral services were to be held at 1:23 p.m. today. Her body was to be laid to rest in a family cemetery which

belief over the slaying. No one can believe it happened."

Witnesses said she got off the bus from Adairsville High School, where she was taking advanced studies, and walked over to talk to man driving a compact car, who forced her into the vehicle and drove away.

The young victim, an exceptionally gifted student, was the daughter of roy and Mary Stoner, who also have a pre-school daughter.

"I can't believe it's happened," Mrs. Stoner said, before her daughter's body was found. "It's something that happens everywhere else, but not here.

In addition to her accelerated studies, the child was described as a friendly and outgoing girl who was captain of the band majorette squad, with first-place awards for baton-twirling. "She was a very talented young lady," said Brent Boulanger, the high school music director. "She was a hard worker. She would rehearse her part, and she did care."

Finding the attacker

Douglas asked the police if they knew anyone who matched the profile. They replied it was an almost perfect match for 24-year-old Darrell Gene Devier, a forestry worker who had been married and divorced twice, but was at the time living with his first ex-wife. He had previously been suspected of raping a 13-year-old girl, but had not been convicted because of lack of evidence. He had served in the army but had been discharged for going absent without leave, and he drove a black Ford Pinto. Moreover, he had been trimming trees along the road which led past Mary Stoner's home at the time of her disappearance, so that the police had already been questioning him as a possible witness rather than a suspect at that early stage.

The problem was his high degree of self-confidence. The police proposed giving him a lie-detector test, but Douglas advised against it, since it was possible he might fool the polygraph, and if so this would only boost his self-confidence still more and make an admission less likely. Instead the strategy was to bring him in for questioning at night, in an apparently more relaxed and less formal setting, with subdued lighting in the interview room. When he arrived at the station, however, he would be interrogated by one representative of the police and another from the FBI who would be identified as such to emphasize the power of the forces being matched against him, and the amount of evidence they already possessed. To reinforce the weight of the case to Devier, the desk was loaded with a mass of files and folders, each with his name on, even though most of them contained sheets of blank paper.

But the most powerful weapon to dent the suspect's confidence was the murder weapon itself. The bloodstained rock was placed on a table in the interrogation room, not directly between suspect and questioners, but at an angle of around 45 degrees to them, so that the suspect would have to turn his head to look at it. This would give the interrogators the chance to watch for high-stress factors which the suspect would find impossible to control, if he were the killer — body language indicating uneasiness, increased sweating, faster breathing, and a more obvious pulse in the carotid artery in his neck.

The line of questioning was deliberately chosen to make it easier for the suspect to talk about the killing, by giving him a means of transferring the blame to his victim. By tentatively implying that she might have led him on, or might have turned on him when events had moved too far, and even that she might have threatened to reveal his identity or to blackmail him, the questioners avoided showing at that stage how much they

disapproved of the crime he had committed. Instead, they were suggesting a degree of sympathy for the position in which he had found himself.

Finding the killer punch

In Douglas' view, the ultimate killer punch from the questioners' point of view was to assume the attacker had been found to have traces of the victim's blood somewhere on his person. Because the suspect would know that bloodstains would have been extremely difficult to avoid with an attack using a weapon like a knife or a blunt object like the rock, it might be possible to convince him that the interrogators already had evidence linking him to the crime, and that all that remained was to fill in the details. In fact, the reason they were asking further questions was to find out WHY he had committed the crime in the first place.

In the case of Devier, the scheme worked perfectly. When he saw the bloodstained rock lying on the table, he turned to look at it, and his breathing and perspiration both increased dramatically. His body language changed from the relaxed, confident demeanor of previous interviews to a more defensive

LEFT
Police officers interrogating a suspect. In addition to the police officers' questioning skills, interrogation tactics and techniques may include careful staging of the level of lighting in the room, the number of files and paperwork on the desk, and the production of any physical evidence that may cause a guilty suspect to react and even confess.

mode. When the matter of the victim's blood was brought up, he started listening intensely, when in Douglas' experience an innocent person would start shouting and protesting innocence.

Finally, Devier not only admitted to the rape, although claiming that his victim had threatened to unmask him, but he admitted to a previous rape for which he had been a suspect. He was tried and convicted of the murder of Mary Frances Stoner and sentenced to death, though his appointment with the electric chair was not until May 18, 1995.

Since then, John Douglas has built up an impressive routine to convey to suspects the resources being marshaled to prove their guilt and the weight of evidence being built up against them. One ploy is to take the suspect through the room which is being used by the investigative task force on the way to their interrogation. The task force room would be full of busy people, with the surfaces packed with case files and the walls decorated with enlargements of photographs of the suspect taken on surveillance operations, or video monitors replaying footage of the suspect from similar sources, all to convince the suspect that if there is

BELOW
Prototype of the serial killer: the body of one of the victims of the scourge of Victorian London's East End slums, Jack the Ripper.

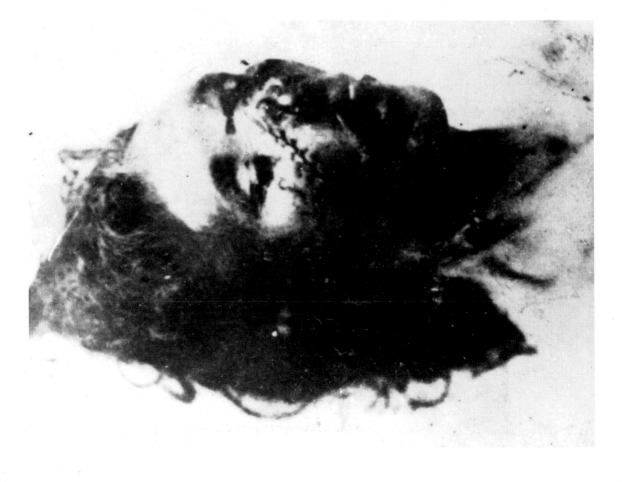

anything he is hoping to keep secret, the police probably know it already. Another useful trigger is to display wall charts which clearly show the kind of penalties the suspect could face if convicted, to increase the pressure on him to confess and plead guilty in the hope of mitigating the sentence he would receive.

Carrying out interrogations late at night or early in the morning can, as in the Devier case, catch suspects when they are at their most relaxed and most vulnerable. These times also carry an additional message that if the interrogation team is happy to work at these unsocial hours, then they are very committed to what they clearly regard as a very serious case. But the key to successful interrogations is to find an equivalent to Devier's bloodstained rock, which will unsettle the suspect and convince him the police already know the most important facts, so he may as well try to put his side of the story in mitigation of the crime they already know he has committed.

Different types — different tactics

Since the early days of using psychological profiling to find the right way to persuade a suspect to reveal the truth, specific techniques have been developed to be effective with different types of criminals. For example, disorganized criminals tend to respond relatively well to questioners appearing to empathize with them and appear to accept whatever stories the suspect tries to tell to distance themselves from the terrible crimes they have committed, until the vital admission of guilt is made. Because this type of criminal is not used to lengthy personal relationships with other people, an effective technique is for the questioners to keep up a constant stream of conversation, suddenly introducing something highly relevant to the crime without warning, to trigger an admission from the suspect which a more leisurely session of questioning might not produce in the same way.

For the more organized criminal, the FBI uses a more directly confrontational technique. Because this type of suspect respects competence and professionalism above all, even when these qualities are being used against their own interests, the interrogators need to present this image with total credibility. However professional they are in reality, though, they must always confine themselves to facts which they know beyond all doubt to be both true and accurate. Any assumption they could get away with saying something is a fact, when the suspect knows it is not, would result in him concluding the investigators had no real case, and that surge of confidence would make it most unlikely he would need to make any incriminating admission at all.

For power-reassurance rapists for example, the main driving force is the need for the criminal to reassure himself of his own masculinity, and any harm done to the victim is very much secondary to this overriding objective. Consequently, interviewers tend to commonly stress the victim's masculinity, and imply that his victim has not suffered unduly as a result of his attack, and emphasize that they realize he had no real wish to cause her more harm than was necessary. By building up a relationship with the criminal, investigators have been able to project themselves into the role of sympathetic advisor or even confessor, to the point where the criminal not only admits to the rape but may also own up to earlier rapes and attacks for which he was ultimately responsible.

For anger-retaliation rapists, the chief driver is their intense hatred for women, so normally it would be essential to ensure the interrogator is male. A variation on this technique which has produced successful results is for the suspect to be questioned initially by a team of one male questioner and one female. When the suspect reacts badly to being questioned by the woman, the male questioner can suggest she leaves the room, and use this small act of co-operation to build up a closer relationship with the suspect, reinforced by the impression he has given of being the dominant partner in this professional male-female set-up, a condition which the suspect would tend to see as a role model.

ABOVE
Rape victims like this 24-year-old woman, commonly find adjustment to normality incredibly difficult.

Trapping the sadists

For power-assertive rapists and killers, the essential quality investigators have to project throughout the interviews is that the case has been prepared meticulously and professionally. All the evidence which places the suspect at the scene of the rape or the killing, all the evidence which links him to the victim, and all other relevant information have between them to be used to build up the impression that the questioners know the suspect carried out the crime, and can prove it. All they are looking for from the suspect is to clear up some of the smaller and more ambiguous details, and in responding to his own tendency to respect people who are meticulous and accurate by helping them to do that, the suspect is effectively admitting his guilt. Although on the face of it the techniques for questioning a suspect may seem to lack the drama of clever profiling to reveal the close and intimate details of the kind of person who committed a horrific and violent crime, they are perhaps even more important in the eventual outcome of a case. Clever profiling can and does often help the hunt for the perpetrator of a crime, but in other cases known suspects, clear physical evidence or local knowledge may well identify a potential killer before the need to work to a profile in aiming the hunt's efforts at the right target.

But in many of these crimes, the victim has been killed so that there are no witnesses who can testify to what actually happened at the scene, and much depends on the killer confessing his guilt. In those circumstances, as well as in those cases where profiling was of decisive importance in helping to reveal the subject, the psychological insights possessed by an experienced and professional profiler may be the best weapon the investigators have. Only by using it to the full can they ensure the truth is finally brought out into the open, and the helpless victims receive justice for their sufferings.

BELOW
Roy Whiting in the interrogation room, shortly before being convicted of the murder and abduction of Sarah Payne in England in 2001. This case brought about Sarah's Law – the action which states that U.K. parents should have access to information on pedophiles living in their local area. Megan's Law, as it is known in the U.S. arose from the rape and murder of Megan Kanka in 1996.

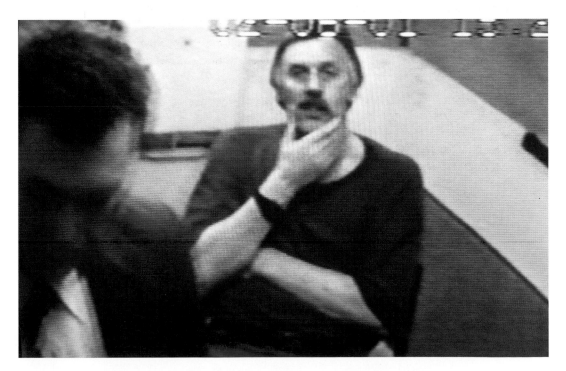

Fred and Rosemary West

House of Death

FRED AND ROSEMARY WEST were almost certainly Britain's most active serial killers. Operating as a depraved but successful husband and wife team, they abducted, sexually abused, and murdered a succession of at least a dozen young girls and women, including among them their own daughter, their children's nanny, and Fred's first wife. Most bodies were then dismembered and buried in various locations, some in secluded fields but most found their last resting places in, beneath, and around the West family home at 25 Cromwell Street in the quiet cathedral city of Gloucester. It was clear that the couple went searching for attractive, young, single women away from home, and persuaded them to accept lifts or hospitality. Working as a couple made it easier to persuade girls on their own to trust them, and once safely back in the house the abuse, torture, and eventual murder of their victims could be carried out at leisure.

It was all too clear from the beginning that both partners in this horrific enterprise must have been willing participants. On some occasions Rosemary would bring back men to the house for sex, with Fred's blessing, as this enabled him to watch and record the encounters through hidden microphones and video cameras. On others, she and Fred would sexually assault their young victims.

Yet interrogators were surprised to find that, although the evidence was all too clear, Fred West was not behaving under questioning as a person with such a psychopathic profile normally would. He admitted his own responsibility, though with explanations chosen to reduce his degree of blame as far as he could, but he refused to admit his wife's involvement in any way at all. The police questioners refused to believe that Rosemary was completely innocent, as Fred claimed. Instead of trying to force him to admit she had

known of the crimes, they changed their tactics. They took him through each of the murders in detail, concentrating on times and dates and other checkable facts, to build up a web of information which would ultimately reveal his partner's guilt, in spite of Fred West's determination to conceal her guilt.

For psychologist and profiler Paul Britton, this obsession of Fred West underlined the value and importance to him of his partner and principal collaborator and his total dependence on her. As a result, if Fred found out Rosemary had subsequently rejected him for any reason or simply came to believe she had forgotten about him during the period of isolation following the initial questioning, he would almost certainly present a serious suicide risk. For the time being, though, Rosemary denied

Fred West, shortly before he hanged himself in his cell while awaiting trial, apparently to protect his wife from prosecution.

Rosemary West denied taking an active part in her husband's crimes.

Profiler Paul Britton who suggested that Fred West's dependence on his wife could result in a suicide attempt if she appeared to turn her back on him following their arrest, a prediction which came true on New Year's Day, 1995.

forthcoming trial canceled for lack of evidence of her direct involvement, on October 6, 1995 she appeared at Winchester Crown Court, charged with ten of the murders including those of a daughter and step-daughter.

Rosemary's trial

Throughout the trial, which lasted almost seven weeks, the defence maintained Rosemary's total ignorance of the crimes with which she had been charged. But the defence made two tactical mistakes. They invited Rosemary West to testify on her own behalf. Because of their careful questioning of Rosemary, the police knew that she had a short temper, and the prosecution were able to use this weakness by subjecting her to an aggressive cross-examination. This tactic provoked her into

all knowledge of, or involvement in, the torture, abuse, murder, and disposal of their victims. When faced with her own step-daughter's evidence of violence and sexual abuse, she simply relied on a flat denial, claiming that her husband had been entirely responsible for the violence in the house.

On the first day of 1995, Fred West was found hanged in his cell at Winson Green prison in Birmingham. He had already been severely shaken when she recoiled from him at their joint hearing. Later, he had written to his children and referred to his anger and disappointment at what he had read in the newspapers which suggested that Rosemary had effectively turned her back on him, and her failure to reply to any of his letters. Though her legal advisers attempted to have Rosemary's

"I Frederick West authorise my solicitor Howard Ogden to advise Supt. Bennett that I wish to admit to a further (approx) 9 killings, expressly Charmaine, Reeha, Linda Gough and others to be identified.

A note from Fred West, dated 4 March 1994, to Detective Superintendent John Bennett admitting to the murders, which his wife Rosemary West was found guilty of, at Winchester Crown Court

revealing damaging facts about the way she had treated her children, and about how she had lied to police in an attempt to cover up the truth. Even more significantly, her loss of temper showed the jury a very different person from the calm, caring, and unaware victim of her husband's deviant behavior she had tried to portray to the court.

The second mistake made by the defence was to play to the jury recordings of Fred West describing how he had committed several of the murders when his wife was out of the house. With advice from those who had carried out the interrogations, the prosecution were able to show that these tapes contained lies on key facts such as dates and times, which revealed that he had been lying in important respects. Once his statements had been effectively discredited, their value as a support for the defence case was largely eliminated.

But the most damaging evidence was provided by a woman who had sat in as a witness on the police questioning of Fred West. Janet Leach testified that Fred West had told her afterwards that Rosemary had murdered his daughter Charmaine and another victim without his being involved, but that he had agreed with his wife that he would take all the blame. This knowledge so preyed on her mind that she had suffered a stroke, and it was only after Fred West's suicide that she had been able to pass on the information to the police. So serious had been the effect of this knowledge on her own health, that she had to be returned to hospital after giving evidence.

Other evidence from Rosemary West's surviving step-daughter, backed up by corroboration from neighbors and potential victims who had managed to escape their clutches, all helped to tear the idea to shreds of her having been an unwitting victim in her own right. Finally, on November 22, the jury convicted Rosemary West on all ten counts of murder, and she was sentenced to life imprisonment, a verdict which was largely due to the careful and methodical interrogation of her husband by the police questioners.

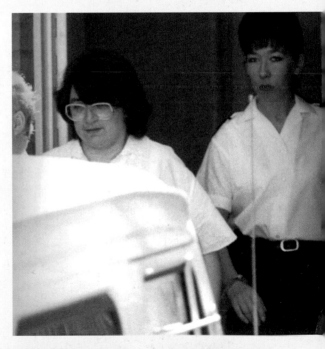

OPPOSITE
The bland exterior of the Wests' home at 25 Cromwell Street, where so many or their victims were buried under floors and in the garden.

ABOVE
Rosemary West, finally convicted of 10 counts of murder and jailed for life.

Catching Karla's killer

Welcome to the Neighborhood

SOMETIMES, INTENSE PSYCHOLOGICAL PRESSURE can be applied to a suspect even before his arrest, both directly and indirectly through other people. Murder victim Karla Brown was 23 years old and engaged to be married to 27-year-old Mark Fair. On June 20, 1978, they threw a party in their new home on Acton Avenue in the little Illinois town of Wood River to celebrate their move. After the party, they returned to the apartment they were moving out of in nearby East Alton to pick up the rest of their belongings. Early the following morning, Mark went to work, and Karla left for the new house, where he was to join her later that afternoon.

LEFT
John Prante, the man convicted of killing Karla Brown. He grew a beard in order to disguise himself to avoid being identified as a suspect.

Mark arrived with a friend of the couple, Tom Fiegenbaum, at around five-thirty, but Karla failed to appear. Mark walked round the back of the house where he found the rear door unlocked. The two men searched the house, and were struck by the fact that items of furniture were overturned. When they looked upstairs, they found Karla kneeling down, wearing only a sweater, with her hands tied behind her back with electrical cable, and her head pushed into a metal drum which had been used for moving clothes, but which was full of water. When they pulled her head from the water and laid her down on the floor, they found she was dead, and immediately called the police.

Despite her head being forced into the water, and in addition to evidence that she had suffered several blows to the head from a blunt instrument, the post mortem revealed she had first been strangled. There was an abundance of fingerprints in the house, but in view of the previous night's party it was almost impossible to determine which, if any, might have belonged to the killer. The only other evidence was provided by witnesses who had seen Karla talking to a "rough-looking man", and by their new next door neighbor Paul Main. He and two friends had been watching the couple move into the apartment, and had hoped to be invited to the party, since one of the three had been at high school with Karla. This friend was later identified as the rough-looking man who had been seen talking to Karla.

LEFT
John Prante, the man convicted of killing Karla Brown. He grew a beard in order to disguise himself to avoid being identified as a suspect.

Expert says bite marks fit Prante

By TERRY HILLIG
Telegraph Staff Writer

Bite marks on the body of Karla Brown, slain in 1978, have been found "consistent" with a dental impression taken from John N. Prante, the man accused of killing her, according to a court document filed in Edwardsville.

An acquaintance of Prante also told an investigator that Prante told him in June, 1978, that he (Prante) had been in Miss Brown's home between 2 and 3 p.m. on the day of her death and that he was a "prime suspect" in the slaying, according to an affidavit by Tom O'Connor, an agent of the Illinois Division of Criminal Investigation.

Prante, 32, of 198 Goulding Ave., East Alton, was arrested Tuesday and charged with murder in the Brown slaying. On Thursday, a grand jury returned an indictment charging Prante with three counts of murder and three counts of burglary in connection with the crime. Prante is being held in the Madison County Jail in Edwardsville. He has been denied bail.

Miss Brown, 22, was found slain on the afternoon of June 21, 1978, in a basement utility room of her home in the 900 block of East Acton Avenue, Wood River. She was found with her hands tied behind her back with electrical cord and her head in a container of water. She had been beaten about the head and face. Authorities believe she drowned.

According to O'Connor's affidavit, apparently filed in support of a petition for a warrant to search Prante's residence, Dr Lowell Levine Tuesday fond Prante's dental impressions consistent with photographs of a bite mark on Miss Brown's body. Prante's dental impressions were taken with his consent on June 4, according to the affidavit.

Levine is a nationally recognized expert in the use of bite marks in criminal investigations. Levine Tuesday also examined dental impressions of two other persons and found them not consistent with the bite marks found on Miss Brown's body, according to the affidavit.

Levine apparently continues to evaluate additional evidence obtained after Miss Brown's body was exhumed last week.

O'Connor also recounted an interview with Spencer Bond , an acquaintance of Prante's, in which Bond said Prante told him in the presence of two other people that he was in Miss Brown's house on the day of the slaying and that he had to get out of town because he was a prime suspect in the slaying, According to the affidavit, Prante left the area after the slaying.

According to O'Connor's affidavit, law enforcement authorities were unaware of bite marks on Miss Brown's body until Dr. Homer Campbell examined photographs of the body in September, 1980.

The affidavit indicated that Spencer Bond said Prante told him in 1978 that Miss Brown had teeth marks on her body.

In asking for the search warrant, investigators said they were seeking an orange T-shirt with Big Bamboo imprinted on the front, a yellow baseball cap, a strand of electrical cord and an end plug and a socket from an extension cord.

In searching Prante's residence Tuesday night, investigators found, among other things, two yellow baseball caps, a rope with knots in it, two photo albums, for "sex magazines," two photographs of an unknown woman and various other photographs and papers, according to the documents.

Paul E. Main Jr., who had been charged with obstructing justice in the case, told investigators Saturday Prante was at his home — next door to the Brown home — on the afternoon of the slaying. Some of the items sought in the search were mentioned by Main.

Main, 26, a Brighton resident, later "directly contradicted" his Saturday statement, according to the criminal information filed against him.

Main, in his statement Saturday, said Prante appeared at his home shortly after he (Main) had noticed a number of police officers arrive at Miss Brown's home: Prante appeared flushed and winded and his T-shirt appeared to have been splashed with water, according to Main.

Main said Prante told him he had to get out of town. He said Prante earlier told him he would like to have sex with Miss Brown and that he knew her, as he had gone to school with her. Main said Saturday he believed Prante killed Karla Brown.

Miss Brown was a former student at Southern Illinois University at Edwardsville, Prante had also been an SIUE student, and threatened female office workers there.

According to O'Connor's affidavit, an FBI expert in preparing criminal profiles theorized that Miss Brown's killer would "probably call the newspapers or authorities and check to see about the case and also be cooperative."

ABOVE
Newspaper coverage of the discovery of evidence which proved John Prante murdered Karla Brown.

The police questioned all potential suspects, giving them lie detector tests which most of them passed. Paul Main and one of his friends, John Prante, were among those tested, though the rough-looking man who had been seen talking to Karla had left the area before the killing and was never seen again. Main's test produced an ambiguous result, though at that stage there was nothing which linked him more positively to the crime. John Prante, however, passed the test completely and at that stage there was nothing more definite to link him to the crime either.

With no other leads to follow, two years passed since the killing with the crime still unsolved. The only positive advance occurred in the summer of 1980 when the local crime scene investigator, Alva Busch, managed to persuade Dr. Homer Campbell, an expert from the University of Arizona in the computer enhancement of photographs, to examine the pictures from both the post-mortem and the crime scene.

Campbell found that marks on the victim's face showed she had been hit with a claw hammer and a small table found close to her body. Even more significant, he found bite marks on her neck, which could potentially be a definite link to her killer. But when Main was given a bite test as a potential suspect following his inconclusive lie-detector test, the result was negative. Once again the investigation came to a halt.

Establishing a profile

Finally, in the spring of 1982, the investigators enlisted the aid of the FBI, who produced a profile with some dramatic implications. Pushing Karla's head into the water was seen as a classic case of staging the crime scene to make it appear different from what it really was. Furthermore, the killer was almost certainly local, and had probably already been interviewed in connection with the killing. The crime was almost certainly unplanned, and probably triggered when the killer made an advance to Karla which she had rejected. To get into the house in the first place, he was probably someone she knew, who had offered to help her with the work of moving in.

The profile also suggested the suspect would be in his middle to late 20s, that he had tried to

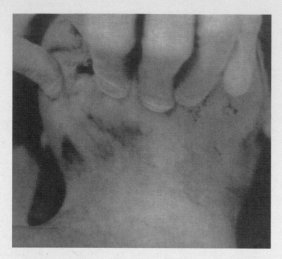

Bites on Karla Brown's neck – a perfect match with John Prante's impression, which ultimately proved his guilt.

have sex with Karla but when she turned him down he had throttled her in a rage. Finding she was apparently unconscious or dead, he had splashed her face with water to try to revive her, and when that failed, he had immersed her head in the water to suggest some kind of bizarre sex game which might have accidentally gone wrong. The profile also suggested that the person involved would be socially and sexually inept, and that he would have low self-esteem, so that drink or drugs would be involved, and may have been drinking heavily to find the courage to make his move. He would also find himself under increasing pressure after the killing, and may well have moved out of the area, though he would try to keep in touch with any progress in the investigation through the local media.

Tracking the killer

As a consequence of the information in the profile, the investigators decided with FBI advice to mount a campaign to flush the killer out of cover. This involved telling the media about the involvement of a profiler, and announcing their intention of exhuming the victim's body to look for additional vital evidence which would trap the person responsible. Undercover agents watched the cemetery to video or photograph any visitors.

When the body was retrieved, the press was told of its excellent state of preservation. Because all this pressure was likely to be causing a reaction from the killer, particular attention had to be paid to reports of anyone behaving strangely or out of character.

Main was still seen as a prime suspect, as he and Prante were known to have been drinking on the day of the killing and were next door to the crime scene. Meanwhile the barrage of publicity about the case produced a call from a witness who knew Karla. The witness, one Martin Higdon, had a colleague at work who had told him she had been to a party soon after the killing, where a man had claimed he had been in Karla's house on the day of her killing, and described her as having been bitten on the shoulder. At that point the police themselves were unaware of the bite mark and so it was not public knowledge.

When police checked with the informant, she revealed the man's name was John Prante. Prante was found to fit the profile in most respects, and witnesses now revealed he had been seen to behave as if under severe stress, with a huge increase in cigarette smoking, the growing of a beard to change his appearance, and finally a move out of the area. He had also taken care to keep up with the progress of the investigation, even asking the first people who interviewed him after the tip-off if they knew what advances had been made.

Finally the police tracked him down, and on June 3, 1982 he was served with a court order to take a bite impression. This produced a perfect match with the bite marks on Karla's neck and a year later he was found guilty of murder and burglary with intent to commit rape, and was sentenced to 75 years in jail.

Index

ACKNOWLEDGEMENTS

Thanking those who helped with the background information; advice and checking of the book is slightly more difficult than usual in this case, as several of those who provided the most valuable input preferred not to be acknowledged by name, including former FBI profilers and current British police officers. Nevertheless, grateful thanks are due to editors Corinne Masciocchi and Ruth Patrick at Quintet, to Duncan Proudfoot who first introduced me to the project, to Geoffrey Thompson for helping to check the text and to the anonymous but ever helpful staff of the Liverpool Reference Libraries. Apologies are due to any other helpers who did not actually prefer to remain anonymous, but were left off the list, and for any errors, responsibility for which are mine.

PICTURE CREDITS

Alton Telegraph p187

Chicago Sun-Times p139 (James Lewis, by Gene Pesek, 1987; Reprinted with special permission from the Chicago Sun-Times, Inc. 2004)

FBI Academy, Quantico p14(b)

Gannet Rochester Newspapers p32, p33(b), p34

Getty Images p1, p2, p9(br), p14(t), p18, p22(b), p25, p27(t), p40(r), p41, p45, p51, p54, p80, p81, p88(t), p99, p103, p111, p125, p134, p141, p162, p173

Journal American Community Newspaper (Predecessor to the King County Journal) p164, p165

The Kobal Collection p8, p9(tl)

Leicester Mercury p102

Madison County Sheriff's Department p186

Gregg McCrary p63

Roy Hazelwood p68

Newark Star Ledger p138, p149

Rex Images p9(tr), p10, p13, p16, p17, p19, p20, p22(t), p23, p24, p28, p31, p33(t), p35, p36, p37, p40(l), p42, p43, p44, p46, p48, p56, p57, p58, p59, p65, p71, p74, p78, p83, p86, p87, p94, p97, p100, p107, p122, p129, p130, p131, p132, p135, p136, p142, p144, p145, p146(t), p147, p150, p152, p153, p154, p155, p158, p159, p166, p167, p168, p169, p170, p181, p184

Richmond Times Dispatch p104, p108, p109, p110, p160

Rome News-Tribune p174, p175

Science Photo Library p64, p66, p171

The State Newspaper p69(l)

Topham Picturepoint p11, p15, p21, p26, p27(b), p30, p38, p61, p62, p63, p69(r), p79, p82, p88(b), p95, p96, p117, p119, p120, p124, p126, p127, p128, p133, p146(b), p157, p177, p178, p180, p182, p183, p185

The Toronto Sun p113, p114, p115

Karen Valentine p53

Wood River Police Department p188

While every effort has been made to credit the relevant parties, the publisher apologises for any omissions.

CRIMINAL MINDS: BIBLIOGRAPHY

The Jigsaw Man, by Paul Britton, London, Corgi Books, 1998.

Profiling Violent Crimes, an Investigative Tool, (3rd edition), Ronald M. Holmes and Stephen T. Holmes, Thousand Oaks, California, SAGE Publications, 2002.

Offender Profiling and Crime Analysis, Peter B. Ainsworth, Portland, Oregon, Willan Publishing, 2001.

Criminal Shadows, David Canter, London, HarperCollins, 1995.

Men who Rape; the Psychology of the Offender, Nicholas Groth, New York, Plenum, 1979.

Serial Murderers and their Victims, E. W. Hickey, California, Brooks-Cole, 1991.

Hunting Humans: the Rise of the Modern Multiple Murderer, E. Leyton, Toronto, Seal Books, 1986

Psychological Methods in Criminal Investigation and Evidence, edited by D. C. Raskin, New York, Springer Publishing, 1989.

Whoever Fights Monsters, R. K. Ressler and T. Schachtman, London, Simon and Schuster, 1992.

The Blooding, Joseph Wambaugh, London, Bantam Books, 1989.

The Anatomy of Motive, John Douglas and Mark Olshaker, London, Simon and Schuster, 2000.

Mindhunter: Inside the FBI Elite Serial Crime Unit, John Douglas and Mark Olshaker, London, Arrow Books, 1997.

The Evil that Men Do, Stephen G. Michaud with Roy Hazelwood, New York, St Martin's Press, 1988.

Signature Killers: Interpreting the Calling Cards of the Serial Murderer, Robert D. Keppel with William J. Birnes, London, Arrow Books, 1998.

Catching the Killers: a History of Crime Detection, James Morton, London, Ebury Press, 2001.

Applying Psychology to Crime, Julie Harrower, London, Hodder & Stoughton, 1998.

Handbook of Psychology for Forensic Practitioners, G. J. Towl and D. A. Crighton, London, Sage, 1996.

Dark Dreams: Sexual Violence, Homicide and the Criminal Mind, Roy Hazelwood and Stephen G. Michaud, New York, St. Martin's Press, 2001.

Sexual Homicide: Patterns and Motives, Robert K. Ressler, Ann W. Burgess and John E. Douglas, London, Simon and Schuster, 1993.

Killers on the Loose, Antonio Mendoza, London, Virgin Books, 2002.

Hidden Evidence, David Owen, London, Time-Life Books, 2000.

Beyond the Crime Lab: the new Science of Investigation, Jon Zonderman, New York, John Wiley & Sons, 1999.

The Casebook of Forensic Detection, Colin Evans, New York, John Wiley & Sons, 1996.

Criminalistics, Richard Saferstein, New York, Prentice Hall (various editions)

The Encyclopaedia of Forensic Science, Brian Lane, London, Hodder Headline, 1992.

She Must Have Known: the Trial of Rosemary West, Brian Masters, London, Corgi Books, 1998.

Practical Aspects of Rape Investigation: a Multidisciplinary Approach, Roy Hazelwood and Ann Burgess (editors), Amsterdam, Elsevier, 1987.

Understanding Sexual Violence: a Study of Convicted Rapists, D Scully, Boston, Unwin Hyman, 1990.

The Scientific Investigation of Crime, S. S. Kind, London, Forensic Science Services Ltd., 1987.

Roadside Prey, Alva Bush, New York, Kensington, 1996.

Crime Classification Manual, John Douglas, Ann Burgess, A. G. Burgess and Robert Ressler, Lexington, MA, Lexington Books, 1992.

The Cases that Haunt Us: From Jack the Ripper to JonBenet Ramsey, the FBI's legendary mindhunter sheds light on the mysteries that won't go away, John Douglas and Mark Olshaker, New York, Scribner, 2000.

The Unknown Darkness — Profiling the Predators among Us, Gregg O. McCrary with Katherine Ramsland PhD, New York, HarperCollins, 2003.

Offender Profiling — Theory, Research and Practice, edited by Janet L. Jackson and Debra A. Bekerian, Chichester (UK), John Wiley, 1997.

Also numerous websites, of which the most useful are: www.criminalprofiling.com and www.crimelibrary.com